OPERA JOURNEYS LIBRETTO SERIES

Mozart's

DON GIOVANNI

TRANSLATED FROM ITALIAN
and including music highlight transcriptions

Edited by Burton D. Fisher
Principal lecturer, *Opera Journeys Lecture Series*

Opera Journeys Publishing™ / Miami, Florida

Opera Journeys™ Mini Guide Series

Opera Classics Library™ Series

Opera Journeys™ Libretto Series

A History of Opera:
Milestones and Metamorphoses

Opera Classics Library PUCCINI COMPANION:
The Glorious Dozen

OVER 60 TITLES AVAILABLE:

L'Africaine   Abduction from the Seraglio   Aida
Andrea Chénier   The Barber of Seville   La Bohème
Boris Godunov   Carmen   Cavalleria Rusticana
Cosi fan tutte   Der Freischütz   Der Rosenkavalier
Die Fledermaus   Don Carlo   Don Giovanni
Don Pasquale   The Elixir of Love   Elektra
Eugene Onegin   Exploring Wagner's Ring   Falstaff
La Fanciulla del West   Faust   La Fille du Régiment
Fidelio   The Flying Dutchman   Gianni Schicchi
Hansel and Gretel   L'Italiana in Algeri   Julius Caesar
Lohengrin   Lucia di Lammermoor   Macbeth
Madama Butterfly   The Magic Flute   Manon
Manon Lescaut   The Marriage of Figaro
A Masked Ball   The Mikado   Norma   Otello
I Pagliacci   Pelléas et Mélisande   Porgy and Bess
The Rhinegold   Rigoletto   The Ring of the Nibelung
La Rondine   Salome   Samson and Delilah   Siegfried
Suor Angelica   Il Tabarro   The Tales of Hoffmann
Tannhäuser   Tosca   La Traviata   Tristan and Isolde
Il Trittico   Il Trovatore   Turandot
Twilight of the Gods   The Valkyrie
Werther   Wozzeck

WEB SITE: www.operajourneys.com   **E MAIL: operaj@bellsouth.net**

DON GIOVANNI

Libretto

ACT I - Scene 1

*A square in Seville. It is night. In front of the palace of the Commandant, Leporello,
holding a lantern, moves about cautiously and impatiently.*

Molto allegro
LEPORELLO

Not - te e   gior - no   fa - ti - car,   per chi   nul - la   sa   gra - dir;

Leporello:
Notte e giorno faticar,
per chi nulla sa gradir,
piova e vento sopportar,
mangiar male e mal dormir.

Voglio far il gentiluomo!
E non voglio più servir.
Oh che caro galantuomo!

Vuol star dentro colla bella,
ed io far la sentinella!
Voglio far il gentiluomo
e non voglio più servir.

Ma mi par che venga gente;
non mi voglio far sentir.

Leporello:
I work hard day and night,
and he never thanks me.
I endure winds and rain,
poor food and little sleep.

I want to be a gentleman!
And I no longer want to be a servant.
Oh what a gallant man!

He's inside with his conquest,
and I am the sentry!
I want to be a gentleman
and I no longer want to be a servant.

But it seems that someone is coming;
I don't want to be seen here.

*As Leporello hides, Don Giovanni enters,
followed by Donna Anna, who holds his arm firmly.*

Donna Anna:
Non sperar, se non m'uccidi,
ch'io ti lasci fuggir mai!

Don Giovanni:
Donna folle! In darno gridi,
chi son io tu non saprai!

Leporello:
Che tumulto! Oh ciel, che gridi!
Il padron in nuovi guai.

Donna Anna:
Gente! Servi! Al traditore!

Donna Anna:
Don't hope, even if you kill me,
I won't let you escape!

Don Giovanni: *(concealing his features)*
Foolish woman! Vain cries!
You'll never know who I am!

Leporello:
What shouting! Heavens, what screaming!
My master's in some new trouble!

Donna Anna:
People! Servants! A traitor!

Don Giovanni:
(Taci e trema al mio furore!)

Don Giovanni: *(covering her mouth)*
(Be silent, or you'll experience my anger!)

Donna Anna:
Scellerato!

Donna Anna:
Villain!

Don Giovanni:
Sconsigliata!

Don Giovanni:
Imprudent woman!

Leporello:
Sta a veder che il malandrino mi farà
precipitar!

Leporello:
Look how this libertine will bring about my
downfall!

Donna Anna:
Come furia disperata ti saprò perseguitar!

Donna Anna:
I'm desperate to know who this pursuer is!

Don Giovanni:
(Questa furia disperata mi vuol far
precipitar!)

Don Giovanni:
(She'll make me do something frightful!)

Donna Anna's father, the Commandant, approaches. Donna Anna rushes into the palace.
The Commandant holds a torch in one hand, and a sword in the other.

Il Commendatore:
Lasciala, indegno! Battiti meco!

Commandant:
Leave her alone! Fight me!

Don Giovanni:
Va, non mi degno di pugnar teco.

Don Giovanni:
Go, I don't want to fight you.

Il Commendatore:
Così pretendi da me fuggir?

Commandant:
Do you think you can get away like a coward?

Leporello:
(Potessi almeno di qua partir!)

Leporello:
(I wish I could get away from here!)

Don Giovanni:
Misero, attendi, se vuoi morir!

Don Giovanni: *(draws his sword)*
Wretch, stand there if you want to die!

The Commandant attacks Don Giovanni.
After Don Giovanni strikes the Commandant with his sword, he falls, mortally wounded.

Il Commendatore:
Ah, soccorso! Son tradito!
L'assassino m'ha ferito,
e dal seno palpitante,
sento l'anima partir.

Commandant:
Ah help! I've been betrayed!
The assassin has wounded me,
and I feel that I am dying.
I feel my soul leaving me.

The Commandant dies. Servants rush from the palace.

Don Giovanni:
Ah, già cade il sciagurato,
affannoso e agonizzante,
già dal seno palpitante
veggo l'anima partir.

Don Giovanni:
The meddling fool lies prostrate,
agonizing and without breath.
His breast throbs,
and I see his soul parting.

Leporello:
Qual misfatto! Qual eccesso!
Entro il sen dallo spavento
palpitar il cor mi sento!
Io non so che far, che dir.

Leporello:
What a horror! What debauchery!
The ghost enters my breast
and I feel my heart throbbing!
I don't know what to do or say.

Don Giovanni and Leporello leave hastily.

Don Giovanni:
Leporello, ove sei?

Don Giovanni: *(in a low voice)*
Leporello, where are you?

Leporello:
Son qui, per mia disgrazia, e voi?

Leporello:
Here, unfortunately. And you?

Don Giovanni:
Son qui.

Don Giovanni:
I'm here.

Leporello:
Chi è morto, voi o il vecchio?

Leporello:
Who's dead, you or the old man?

Don Giovanni:
Che domanda da bestia! Il vecchio.

Don Giovanni:
What a foolish question! The old man.

Leporello:
Bravo, due imprese leggiadre!
Sforzar la figlia ed ammazzar il padre!

Leporello:
Great, two impressive exploits!
Seduce the daughter, and murder the father!

Don Giovanni:
L'ha voluto, suo danno.

Don Giovanni:
He willed his ruin.

Leporello:
Ma Donn'Anna, cosa ha voluto?

Leporello:
And did Donna Anna will her's too?

Don Giovanni:
Taci, non mi seccar, vien meco, se non vuoi
qualche cosa ancor tu!

Don Giovanni: *(threatening Leporello)*
Quiet, don't question me.
Come with me unless you want the same fate!

Leporello:
Non vo'nulla, Signor, non parlo più.

Leporello:
I want nothing. Sir, I'll say no more.

Both Don Giovanni and Leporello depart.

In agitation, Donna Anna and Don Octavio descend the palace steps.
They are followed by servants bearing torches.

Donna Anna:
Ah, del padre in periglio in soccorso voliam.

Donna Anna:
Ah, my father is in danger, let's hurry to help him.

Don Ottavio:
Tutto il mio sangue verserò, se bisogna.
Ma dov'è il scellerato?

Don Octavio: *(raising his sword)*
I'll shed my last drop of my blood, if necessary. But where is the scoundrel?

Donna Anna:
In questo loco. Ma qual mai s'offre.

Donna Anna:
Here in the palace.

Donna Anna sees her father, and throws herself on the corpse.

O Dei, spettacolo funesto agli occhi miei!
Il padre! Padre mio! Mio caro padre!

But heavens, what a horrible sight before me! Father! My dear father!

Don Ottavio:
Signore!

Don Octavio:
My lord!

Donna Anna:
Ah, l'assassino mel trucidò.
Quel sangue, quella piaga, quel volto,
tinto, e coperto del color di morte,
ei non respira più fredde ha le membra
padre mio!
Caro padre! Padre amato! Io manco, io moro.

Donna Anna:
Ah, the assassin murdered him.
That blood, the wound, his face covered and stained. He has the pallor of death.
My father! He no longer breathes, and his limbs are cold! Dear father!
Beloved father! I am fainting. I am dying.

Donna Anna faints momentarily, and then Don Octavio raises her and seats her.

Don Ottavio:
Ah, soccorrete, amici, il mio tesoro!
Cercatemi, recatemi qualche odor, qualche spirito.
Ah! Non tardate. Donn'Anna! Sposa!
Amica! Il duolo estremo la meschinella uccide.

Don Octavio: *(calling servants)*
My friends, help me with my beloved!
Fetch water, some scents, some spirits.

Please hurry. Donna Anna! My beloved!
Her intense grief is destroying her.

Donna Anna:
Ahi!

Donna Anna: *(after being restored by smelling salts) Ah*, me!

Don Ottavio:
Già rinviene. Datele nuovi aiuti.

Don Octavio:
She's reviving. Give her more help.

Donna Anna:
Padre mio!

Donna Anna: *(sighing despairingly)*
My father!

Don Ottavio:
Celate, allontanate agli occhi suoi
quell'oggetto d'orrore. Anima mia,
consolati, fa core.

Don Octavio: *(to the servants)*
Quickly remove her from this scene of
horror. Dear love, console yourself and be
strong.

Servants remove the Commandant's body into the palace.

Allegro
DONNA ANNA

Fug - gi, crudele, fuggi! la - scia, che mora an - ch'io

Donna Anna:
Fuggi, crudele, fuggi!
Lascia che mora anch'io
ora che è morto, oh Dio!
Chi a me la vita diè!

Donna Anna: *(repulsing Don Octavio)*
Leave me, cruel man, leave me!
Let me die too!
Oh God, the man who brought me life
is now dead!

Don Ottavio:
Senti, cor mio, deh! Senti;
guardami un solo istante!
Ti parla il caro amante,
che vive sol per te.

Don Octavio:
Listen, my beloved, listen!
Look at me for just one moment!
Your dear lover speaks to you,
the man who lives only for you.

Donna Anna:
Tu sei! Perdon, mio bene.
L'affanno mio, le pene.
Ah! Il padre mio dov'è?

Donna Anna: *(apologetically)*
You are indeed my love! Forgive me!
I have such anguish and pain.
Ah! Father where are you?

Don Ottavio:
Il padre?
Lascia, o cara, la rimembranza amara.
Hai sposo e padre in me.

Don Octavio:
Your father?
Abandon that bitter thought.
You have both husband and father in me.

Donna Anna:
Ah! Vendicar, se il puoi,
giura quel sangue ognor!

Donna Anna: *Creepy?*
If you can avenge me,
swear it on this honorable blood!

Don Ottavio:
Lo giuro agli occhi tuoi, lo giuro al nostro
amor!

Don Octavio: *(raising his hand as if
taking an oath)* I swear it before your eyes.
I swear it by our love!

A due:
Che giuramento, o dei!
Che barbaro momento!
Tra cento affetti e cento vammi
ondeggiando il cor.

Both:
That us our vow, oh Gods!
What a horrible moment!
So much emotion and grief
stir in my heart.

Both enter the palace.

ACT I - Scene 2

A street in Seville. It is early morning.

Don Giovanni:
Orsù, spicciati presto. Cosa vuoi?

Don Giovanni:
Hurry up. What do you want?

Leporello:
L'affar di cui si tratta è importante.

Leporello:
What I am about to speak about is important.

Don Giovanni:
Lo credo.

Don Giovanni:
No doubt.

Leporello:
È importantissimo.

Leporello:
It's very important.

Don Giovanni:
Meglio ancora. Finiscila.

Don Giovanni:
Better yet. Get to the point.

Leporello:
Giurate di non andar in collera.

Leporello:
Swear not to get angry.

Don Giovanni:
Lo giuro sul mio onore, purché non parli del Commendatore.

Don Giovanni:
I swear it on my honor, as long as you don't mention the Commandant.

Leporello:
Siamo soli?

Leporello:
Are we alone?

Don Giovanni:
Lo vedo.

Don Giovanni:
I believe so.

Leporello:
Nessun ci sente?

Leporello:
No one can hear us?

Don Giovanni:
Via!

Don Giovanni:
Go ahead!

Leporello:
Vi posso dire tutto liberamente?

Leporello:
Can I speak freely?

Don Giovanni:
Sì.

Don Giovanni:
You may.

Leporello:
Dunque quando è così, caro signor padrone, la vita che menate è da briccone!

Leporello:
Well, if that's the case, my dear master, the life you are leading is disgraceful!

Don Giovanni:
Temerario, in tal guisa!

Leporello:
E il giuramento!

Don Giovanni:
Non so di giuramenti. Taci, o ch'io...

Leporello:
Non parlo più, non fiato, o padron mio!

Don Giovanni:
Così saremo amici. Ora dì un poco: sai tu
perché son qui?

Leporello:
Non ne so nulla.
Ma essendo l'alba chiara, non sarebbe
qualche nuova conquista?
Io lo devo saper per porla in lista.

Don Giovanni:
Va là, che sei il grand'uom!
Sappi ch'io sono innamorato d'una bella
dama, e son certo che m'ama.
La vidi, le parlai; meco al casino questa
notte verrà.
Zitto, mi pare sentire odor di femmina!

Leporello:
(Cospetto, che odorato perfetto!)

Don Giovanni:
All'aria mi par bella.

Leporello:
(E che occhio, dico!)

Don Giovanni:
Ritiriamoci un poco, e scopriamo terren.

Leporello:
(Già prese foco!)

Don Giovanni:
How dare you talk to me that way!

Leporello:
But you promised!

Don Giovanni: *(threateningly)*
I know of no promises. Quiet, or I....

Leporello:
Master, I'll say no more, not another breath!

Don Giovanni:
So now we can be friends. Listen, do you
know why I'm here?

[handwritten: sudden!]

Leporello:
I've no idea.
But it's a clear morning. Do you have
some new conquest? You must tell me the
lady's name so I can put her in my list.

Don Giovanni:
Spoken like an intelligent man!
You must know that I'm in love with a
most beautiful woman, and I'm sure she
loves me. I've seen her and talked to her.
She's to meet me at the country house.
Quiet, I seem to smell the aroma of a woman!

Leporello:
(Wow, what a perfect sense of smell!)

Don Giovanni:
Her fragrance seems to be beautiful.

Leporello:
(And what an eye he has!)

Don Giovanni:
Let's hide ourselves for a while, and
check things out.

Leporello:
(He's already on fire!)

As Don Giovanni and Leporello conceal themselves, Donna Elvira approaches.

Allegro
DONNA ELVIRA

Ah! chi mi di - ce ma - i,   quel   bar - baro   dov'è?

Donna Elvira:
Ah, chi mi dice mai
quel barbaro dov'è,
che per mio scorno amai,
che mi mancò di fe?

Ah, se ritrovo l'empio
e a me non torna ancor,
vo' farne orrendo scempio,
gli vo' cavare il cor.

Don Giovanni:
Udisti? Qualche bella dal vago
abbandonata.
Poverina! Cerchiam di consolare il suo
tormento.

Leporello:
(Così ne consolò mile e ottocento).

Don Giovanni:
Signorina! Signorina!

Donna Elvira:
Chi è là?

Don Giovanni:
Stelle! Che vedo!

Leporello:
(O bella! Donna Elvira!)

Donna Elvira:
Don Giovanni! Sei qui?
Mostro! Fellon! Nido d'inganni!

Donna Elvira:
Ah, who will tell me
where that traitor is?
How could I love such a man
who betrayed my faith?

But if I find the traitor,
and if he doesn't return to me,
I'll inflict havoc on him,
and tear his heart out.

Don Giovanni: *(softly to Leporello)*
Do you hear? This fair damsel is
complaining of some faithless lover.
Poor girl! I must try to console her anguish.

Leporello:
(Like the way he consoled one thousand
eight hundred!)

Don Giovanni: *(boldly approaching
Donna Elvira) Miss!* Miss!

Donna Elvira:
Who is there?

Don Giovanni:
Good Heavens! Who do I see?

Leporello:
(Oh, it's the beautiful Donna Elvira!)

Donna Elvira:
Don Giovanni! You here!
Monster! Criminal! Deceiver!

Leporello:
(Che titoli cruscanti!
Manco male che lo conosce bene!)

Don Giovanni:
Via, cara Donna Elvira, calmate quella
collera! Sentite, lasciatemi parlar!

Donna Elvira:
Cosa puoi dire, dopo azion sì nera?
In casa mia entri furtivamente.
A forza d'arte, di giuramenti e di lusinghe
arrivi a sedurre il cor mio; m'innamori, o
crudele!

Mi dichiari tua sposa, e poi, mancando della
terra e del ciel al santo dritto,
con enorme delitto dopo tre dì da Burgos
t'allontani.
M'abbandoni, mi fuggi, e lasci in preda al
rimorso ed al pianto, per pena forse che
t'amai cotanto!

Leporello:
(Pare un libro stampato!)

Don Giovanni:
Oh, in quanto a questo, ebbi le mie ragioni!
È vero?

Leporello:
È vero! E che ragioni forti!

Donna Elvira:
E quali sono, se non la tua perfidia, la
leggerezza tua? Ma il giusto cielo volle
ch'io ti trovassi, per far le sue, le mie
vendette.

Don Giovanni:
Eh via! Siate più ragionevole!
(Mi pone a cimento costei!)
Se non credete a labbro mio, credete a
questo galantuomo.

Leporello:
(Salvo il vero.)

Leporello:
(What choice epithets!
She certainly knows him well!)

Don Giovanni:
Come, dear Elvira, calm your fury!
Listen, let me speak!

Donna Elvira:
What can you say after such awful
behavior? You entered my house secretly.
You used cunning, flattery, and promises to
seduce my heart; I fell in love with you, you
cruel man!

You declared me your wife, and then, you
defied the holy laws of heaven and earth
and denied my sacred right; after three
days you abandoned me in Burgos. You
abandoned me, you fled, and left me in
remorse and tears, my punishment because
I loved you so much!

Leporello:
(She echoes the printed romances!)

Don Giovanni:
As to those concerns, I had my reasons for
doing it! Didn't I, Leporello?

Leporello: *(ironically)*
You certainly did! Very important reasons!

Donna Elvira:
What can they be other than your perfidy
and reckless inconsideration? But the
righteous heavens wanted me to find you,
to impose their revenge and mine.

Don Giovanni:
Come now! Be more reasonable!
(This woman embarrasses me!)
If you don't believe me, believe this
trustworthy gentleman.

Leporello:
(I'll vow the truth.)

Don Giovanni:
Via, dille un poco.

Don Giovanni:
Come here and tell her something.

Leporello:
E cosa devo dirle?

Leporello: *(aside to Giovanni)*
And what am I to tell her?

Don Giovanni:
Sì, sì, dille pur tutto.

Don Giovanni:
Yes, yes, explain everything.

Donna Elvira does not notice that Don Giovanni has fled.

Donna Elvira:
Ebben, fa presto!

Donna Elvira: *(to Leporello)*
Well, tell me right away!

Leporello:
Madama, veramente, in questo mondo
conciò, sia cosa, quando, fosse che, il
quadro non è tondo.

Leporello: *(hesitating)*
Madam, truthfully, most assuredly in the
strange world in which we live, it may be
safely asserted that a square is not a circle.

Donna Elvira:
Sciagurato! Così del mio dolor giuoco?
Ti prendi? Ah voi!

Donna Elvira:
You scoundrel! Are you mocking my
grief? And you, Don Giovanni.

Donna Elvira suddenly discovers that Don Giovanni has gone.

Stelle! L'iniquo fuggì! Misera me! Dov'è?
In qual parte?

Heavens! The wicked one fled! Poor me!
Where is he? Which way did he go?

Leporello:
Eh! Lasciate che vada. Egli non merita che
di lui ci pensiate.

Leporello:
Ah, let him go! He doesn't deserve your
thoughts.

Donna Elvira:
Il scellerato m'ingannò, mi tradì.

Donna Elvira:
The scoundrel deceived and betrayed me!

Leporello:
Eh! Consolatevi; non siete voi,
non foste, e non sa retenè la prima,
né l'ultima.

Leporello:
Console yourself! You are not the first
woman he has deserted,
And neither will you be the last.

Guardate: questo non picciol libro è tutto
pieno dei nomi di sue belle.
Ogni villa, ogni borgo, ogni paese è
testimon di sue donnesche imprese.

Look! This large book is filled entirely
with the names of his conquests.
Every village, every town, and every
country has witnessed his impressive exploits.

Leporello takes a large list from his pocket:
the catalog of Don Giovanni's exploits.

Allegro
LEPORELLO

Ma - da - mi - na!   Il ca-ta - lo-go è questo,

Madamina! Il catalogo è questo	Dear little lady! This is the catalog
delle belle che amò il padron mio;	of the beautiful women my master has
un catalogo egli è che ho fatt'io;	loved; a catalog I made myself.
osservate, leggete con me!	Look at it, and read it with me!
In Italia seicento e quaranta;	In Italy 640;
in Almagna duecento e trent'una;	in Germany 231;
cento in Francia, in Turchia novantina;	100 in France, and in Turkey 91;
ma in Ispagna son già mille e tre!	but in Spain, there are already 1003!
V'han fra queste contadine,	Among these, there are peasant girls,
cameriere, cittadine.	waitresses, and town girls.
V'han contesse, baronesse,	There are Countesses and Baronesses,
Marchesine, principesse.	Marchionesses and Princesses.
E v'han donne d'ogni grado,	There have been women of every rank,
d'ogni forma, d'ogni età!	every shape, and every age!
Nella bionda egli ha l'usanza	With the blond women, it's his custom
di lodar la gentilezza.	to praise their gentleness.
Nella bruna la costanza,	With the dark haired, their fidelity,
nella bianca la dolcezza.	and with the gray haired, their sweetness.
Vuol d'inverno la grassotta,	In winter he wants them plump,
vuol d'estate la magrotta.	But in summer he wants them lean.
È la grande maestosa,	He is always charming to the big ladies
la piccina e ognor vezzosa.	as well as the small.
Delle vecchie fa conquista	He conquers the old ones
pel piacer di porle in lista.	for the pleasure of adding them to the list.
Sua passion predominante	But his predominant passion
è la giovin principiante.	is the young beginner.
Non si pica, se sia ricca,	He doesn't mind if she's rich,
se sia brutta, se sia bella.	or ugly, or beautiful.
Purché porti la gonnella,	You know what he does,
voi sapete quel che fa.	providing she wears a skirt.

Method / His ways

Leporello leaves hastily.

Donna Elvira:
In questa forma dunque mi tradì il
scellerato!

Donna Elvira:
This is the way that scoundrel betrayed me!

È questo il premio che quel barbaro rende all'amor mio?
Ah! Vendicar vogl'io l'ingannato mio cor!
Pria ch'ei mi fugga si ricorra, si vada,
io sento in petto sol vendetta parlar, rabbia e dispetto!

Is this the way that barbarian returns my affection?
Ah! I want revenge for my deceived heart!
Before he escapes me, I'll have recourse.
I feel only revenge in my heart, rage and malice!

Elvira departs.

ACT I - Scene 3

The open country with a view of Don Giovanni's palace.
Zerlina, Masetto, and a group of peasants sing and dance.

Zerlina:
Giovinette che fate all'amore,
non lasciate che passi l'età!
Se nel seno vi bulica il core,
il rimedio vedetelo qua!
Fa la la, la la la, la la la!
Che piacer, che piacer che sarà!

Zerlina:
Pretty lasses, indulge in love,
and don't let your youth fly by!
If the flames burn in your heart,
the remedy is here!
Fa la la, la la la, la la la!
What pleasure, what pleasure there will be!

Coro:
Ah, che piacer, che piacer che sarà!
Fa la la...

Chorus:
What pleasure, what pleasure there will be!
Fa la la....

Masetto:
Giovinetti leggeri di testa,
non andate girando di là.
Poco dura de'matti la festa,
ma per me cominciato non ha.
Fa la la, la la la, la la la!
Che piacer, che piacer che sarà!

Masetto:
Boys, don't keep spinning around because your heads will not be clear.
The mad party will last a while,
but for me, it hasn't begun.
Fa la la, la, la la, la la la!
What pleasures, what pleasure there will be!

Zerlina e Masetto:
Vieni, vieni, carino, godiamo,
e cantiamo e balliamo e suoniamo!
Che piacer, che piacer che sarà!

Zerlina and Masetto:
Come, come, dearest, let's enjoy ourselves,
and let's sing, dance, and dream!
What pleasure, what pleasure there will be!

Coro:
Fa la la, la la la, la la la!
Che piacer, che piacer che sarà!

Chorus:
Fa la la, la la la, fa la la!
What pleasure, what pleasure there will be!

Don Giovanni and Leporello arrive.

Don Giovanni:
(Manco male, è partita.)
Oh guarda, che bella gioventù; che belle
donne!

Don Giovanni:
(Thank God, she is gone.)
Look, what beautiful young and pretty
girls!

Leporello:
(Fra tante, per mia fè, vi sarà qualche cosa
anche per me.)

Leporello:
(I have faith that soon one of them might be
for me.)

Don Giovanni:

Cari amici, buon giorno! Seguitate a stare
allegramente, seguite a suonar, buona
gente! C'è qualche sposalizio?

Don Giovanni:
(interrupting Zerlina and Masetto)
Dear friends, good morning! Good people,
continue to enjoy yourselves and continue
to play! Is there going to be a wedding?

Zerlina:
Sì, signore, e la sposa son io.

Zerlina: *(bowing politely to Don Giovanni)*
Yes, sir, and I am the bride.

Don Giovanni:
Me ne consolo. Lo sposo?

Don Giovanni:
I'm happy for you. Where is the bridegroom?

Masetto:
Io, per servirla.

Masetto:
Here, at your service.

Don Giovanni:
Oh bravo! Per servirmi; questo è vero parlar
da galantuomo.

Don Giovanni:
How wonderful! Spoken like a gallant man
who serves me.

Leporello:
(Basta che sia marito!)

Leporello:
(As long as he remains the husband and
not the cuckold!)

Zerlina:
Oh, il mio Masetto è un uom d'ottimo core.

Zerlina:
Oh, my dear Masetto is such a generous man.

Don Giovanni:
Oh anch'io, vedete!
Voglio che siamo amici. Il vostro nome?

Don Giovanni:
And be assured, I see it! Let's be friends.
What is your name?

Zerlina:
Zerlina.

Zerlina;
Zerlina.

Don Giovanni:
E il tuo?

Don Giovanni: *(to Masetto)*
And yours?

Masetto:
Masetto.

Don Giovanni:
O caro il mio Masetto!
Cara la mia Zerlina!
V'esibisco la mia protezione.

Don Giovanni looks for Leporello, who is among the peasant girls.

Leporello! Cosa fai lì, birbone?

Leporello:
Anch'io, caro padrone, esibisco la mia
protezione.

Don Giovanni:
Presto, va con costor; nel mio palazzo
conducili sul fatto: ordina ch'abbiano
cioccolatta, caffè, vini, prosciutti; cerca
divertir tutti, mostra loro il giardino, la
galleria, le camere; in effetto fa che resti
contento il mio Masetto. Hai capito?

Leporello:
Ho capito. Andiam!

Masetto:
Signore!

Don Giovanni:
Cosa c'è?

Masetto:
La Zerlina senza me non può star.

Leporello:
In vostro loco ci sarà sua eccellenza; e saprà
bene fare le vostre parti.

Don Giovanni:
Oh, la Zerlina è in man d'un cavalier.
Va pur, fra poco ella meco verrà.

Zerlina:
Va! Non temere! Nelle mani son io d'un
cavaliere.

Masetto:
Masetto.

Don Giovanni:
Ah my dear Masetto!
My dear Zerlina!
I am pleased to offer you my protection.

Leporello, you knave! What are you doing
over there?

Leporello:
I too, dear master, am offering my
protection.

Don Giovanni:
Hurry, and take these happy people to my
palace: order chocolate, coffee, wine, ham.
Find a way to entertain them; show them
the garden, the gallery, the rooms, and
above all, make sure that my dear Masetto
is happy. Do you understand?

Leporello:
I understand. *(to Masetto)* Let's go!

Masetto:
Sir!

Don Giovanni:
What is it?

Masetto:
Zerlina can't stay here without me.

Leporello: *(to Masetto)*
His excellency will take your place; he
knows well how to play your part.

Don Giovanni:
Zerlina is in the care of a nobleman. Go
then! She'll soon return with me.

Zerlina:
Go! Don't worry! I am in the hands of a
nobleman.

Masetto:
E per questo?

Masetto:
And for what reason?

Zerlina:
E per questo non c'è da dubitar

Zerlina:
Because there's no reason to worry.

Masetto:
Ed io, cospetto.

Masetto: *(trying to take Zerlina's hand)*
And what about me?

Don Giovanni:
Olà, finiam le dispute! Se subito senza altro replicar non te ne vai, Masetto, guarda ben, ti pentirai!

Don Giovanni: *(stepping between them)*
Now, the dispute is over! Masetto, be careful! If you don't leave immediately and without arguing, you'll regret it!

Masetto:
Ho capito, signor sì!
Chino il capo e me ne vo.
Già che piace a voi così,
altre repliche non fo.

Masetto: *(dumbfounded)*
I understand sir, yes!
I just bow my head and go.
As you wish,
and no further argument.

Cavalier voi siete già.
Dubitar non posso affè;
me lo dice la bontà
che volete aver per me.

You are indeed a cavalier.
I cannot doubt it.
You tell me how kind
you want to be with me.

Bricconaccia, malandrina!
Fosti ognor la mia ruina!

(aside to Zerlina)
Little cheat! Viper!
You were born to be my ruin!

(Leporello forces Masetto away)
Vengo, vengo!

(Leporello forces Masetto away)
I'm coming, I'm coming!

Resta, resta.
È una cosa molto onesta!
Faccia il nostro cavaliere ancora te.

(to Zerlina)
Stay, stay. It's quite prudent to trust him!
Let this nobleman also make a lady of you.

Leporello hurries Masetto into the tavern.

Don Giovanni:

Alfin siam liberati, Zerlinetta gentil, da quel scioccone. Che ne dite, mio ben, so far pulito?

Don Giovanni:
(trying to embrace Zerlina)
My gentle little Zerlina, at last we are free of that troublesome fellow. Tell me, my angel, didn't I handle it well?

Zerlina:
Signore, è mio marito!

Zerlina:
But Sir, he is my fiancé!

Don Giovanni:
Chi? Colui?

Vi par che un onest'uomo, un nobil cavalier, com'io mi vanto, possa soffrir che quel visetto d'oro, quel viso inzuccherato da un bifolcaccio vil sia strapazzato?

Zerlina:
Ma, signore, io gli diedi parola di sposarlo.

Don Giovanni:
Tal parola non vale un zero. Voi non siete fatta per essere paesana; un altra sorte vi procuran quegli occhi bricconcelli, quei labretti sì belli, quelle dituccie candide e odorose, parmi toccar giuncata e fiutar rose.

Zerlina:
Ah! Non vorrei.

Don Giovanni:
Che non vorreste?

Zerlina:
Alfine ingannata restar. Io so che raro colle donne voi altri cavalieri siete onesti e sinceri.

Don Giovanni:
È un impostura della gente plebea! La nobiltà ha dipinta negli occhi l'onestà. Orsù, non perdiam tempo; in questo istante io ti voglio sposar.

Zerlina:
Voi?

Don Giovanni:

Certo, io. Quel casinetto è mio: soli saremo e là, gioiello mio, ci sposeremo.

Don Giovanni:
Who! Him?
Do you think that an honest nobleman, a man of rank like me, can bear to see this such precious and sweet face snatched away by a plowman?

Zerlina:
But sir, I have promised to marry him.

Don Giovanni:
Such a promise means nothing. You were not born to be country wife. Those roguish eyes deserve another destiny. Those beautiful lips, those white-scented fingers, are like touching cream and sniffing roses.

Zerlina:
Ah! I don't want to.

Smooth talker

Don Giovanni:
What don't you want?

appearance / vs. reality

Zerlina:
To be deceived in the end. I know that noblemen are seldom frank and honest with women.

Don Giovanni:
It is a popular fiction of the common people! The nobility has honesty painted in its eyes. But let's not waste time: I want to marry you right away.

Zerlina:
You?

Don Giovanni:
(pointing to the country house) Certainly. That little house you see is mine. My treasure, there we can be alone, and there we will be married.

Andante
DON GIOVANNI

Là   ci da - rem la ma-no,   là   mi di - rai di   sì,

Là ci darem la mano,
là mi dirai di sì.
Vedi, non è lontano; partiam,
ben mio, da qui.

There, we'll take each other's hand,
and there, you will say yes.
Look, it isn't far.
Let's go, my love, let's go from here.

Zerlina:
(Vorrei e non vorrei,
mi trema un poco il cor.
Felice, è ver, sarei,
ma può burlarmi ancor!)

Zerlina:
(I would like to, and I wouldn't like to.
My heart is trembling a little.
It's true, I'd be happy,
unless this nobleman deceives me!)

Don Giovanni:
Vieni, mio bel diletto!

Don Giovanni:
Come, my beautiful treasure!

Zerlina:
(Mi fa pietà Masetto!)

Zerlina:
(I feel sorry for Masetto!)

Don Giovanni:
Io cangierò tua sorte!

Quickly under his spell

Don Giovanni:
I will change your fate!

Zerlina:
Presto, non son più forte!

Zerlina:
I feel myself weakening so quickly!

Don Giovanni:
Vieni, vieni! Andiam! Andiam!

Don Giovanni:
Come, come! Let's go! Let's go!

Zerlina:
Andiam!

Zerlina:
Let's go!

A due:
Andiam, andiam, mio bene
a ristorar le pene
s'un innocente amor!

Together:
Let's go, let's go, my love
to share the pleasure
of innocence and love!

Donna Elvira has been watching Don Giovanni and Zerlina.
As Don Giovanni and Zerlina walk toward the little house (casino),
Donna Elvira blocks their passage.

Donna Elvira:
Fermati, scellerato! Il ciel mi fece udir le tue
perfidie!
Io sono a tempo di salvar questa misera
innocente dal tuo barbaro artiglio!

Donna Elvira:
Stop, scoundrel! Heaven made me hear
your perfidious behavior!
I have arrived just in time to save this poor
innocent girl from your barbaric clutches!

Zerlina:
Meschina! Cosa sento!

Zerlina:
Oh, my! What I am hearing!

Don Giovanni:
(Amor, consiglio!)
Idol mio, non vedete ch'io voglio
divertirmi?

Don Giovanni:
(Cupid, advise me!) *(softly to Elvira)*
My love, don't you see that I am amusing
myself?

Donna Elvira:
Divertirti, è vero? Divertirti, io so, crudele,
come tu ti diverti.

Donna Elvira:
Amusing yourself? Yes, cruel man, I know
too well how you amuse yourself.

Zerlina:
Ma, signor cavaliere, è ver quel ch'ella dice?

Zerlina: *(anxiously to Don Giovanni)*
But, my lord, is this lady telling the truth?

Don Giovanni:
La povera infelice è di me innamorata, e per
pietà deggio fingere amore, ch'io son, per
mia disgrazia, uom di buon cuore.

Don Giovanni: *(softly to Zerlina)*
The poor unhappy women is in love with me,
and out of pity I pretend to love her. That is
my misfortune. I am so kind-hearted.

After Don Giovanni departs, Donna Elvira admonishes Zerlina.

What an ass!

Allegro
DONNA ELVIRA

Ah! fug - gi il tra - di - tor!   Non lo lasciar   più dir;

Donna Elvira:
Ah, fuggi il traditor!
Non lo lasciar più dir!
Il labbro è mentitor,
fallace il ciglio!

Donna Elvira:
Escape from this traitor!
Don't let him say anything more!
His words are all lies,
and deception is in his eyes!

Da' miei tormenti impara
a creder a quel cor,
e nasca il tuo timor
dal mio periglio!

Learn from my torment,
and believe my heart.   → Learn from another's experience!
And let my misfortune
arouse your fear!

Donna Elvira leads Zerlina away.

Don Giovanni:
Mi par ch'oggi il demonio si diverta
d'opporsi a miei piacevoli progressi vanno
mal tutti quanti.

Don Giovanni:
It seems that today the devil enjoys himself
by opposing my pursuit of pleasures. All my
schemes are going badly.

Don Octavio and Donna Anna appear.

Don Ottavio:
Ah! Ch'ora, idolo mio, son vani i pianti,
di vendetta si parli!
Oh, Don Giovanni!

Don Octavio:
Dearest Donna Anna, those tears are in
vain, when you speak only of revenge!
Oh, Don Giovanni!

Don Giovanni:
(Mancava questo intoppo!)

Don Giovanni:
(And now this unfortunate encounter!)

Donna Anna:
Signore, a tempo vi ritroviam.
Avete core?
Avete anima generosa?

Donna Anna:
Sir, we have found you at an opportune
time. Do you have a good heart?
Do you have a generous soul?

Don Giovanni:
(Sta a vedere che il diavolo gli ha detto
qualche cosa.)
Che domanda! Perchè?

Don Giovanni:
(I wonder whether the devil has told her
something.) What a question, Madame!
Why do you ask it?

Donna Anna:
Bisogno abbiamo della vostra amicizia.

Donna Anna:
We have need of your friendship.

Don Giovanni:
(Mi torna il fiato in corpo.)
Comandate. I congiunti, i parenti, questa
man, questo ferro, i beni, il sangue
spenderò per servirvi.
Ma voi, bella Donn'Anna, perchè così
piangete? Il crudele chi fu che osò la calma
turbar del viver vostro?

Don Giovanni:
(I breathe again.)
Command me. My kinsmen, my relations,
this arm, my sword, my wealth, my blood:
all are at your service. But you, beautiful
Donna Anna, why are you crying? Who is
the wretch who has dared to disturb your
peaceful life?

Donna Elvira enters.

Donna Elvira:
Ah, ti ritrovo ancor, perfido mostro! Non ti
fidar, o misera, di quel ribaldo cor! Me già
tradì quel barbaro, te vuol tradir ancor.

Donna Elvira: *(to Don Giovanni)*
Ah, I find you again, you perfidious
monster! (to *Donna Anna*) Sad lady, do not
confide in this rogue! This barbarian has
already betrayed me, and he wants to betray
you too.

Donna Anna e Don Ottavio:
(Cieli, che aspetto nobile!
Che dolce maestà! Il suo pallor, le lagrime
m'empiono di pietà.)

Donna Anna and Don Octavio:
(Heavens, what a noble bearing she has!
What gentle grace! Her ashen face and her
tears, fill me with pity.)

Don Giovanni:
La povera ragazza è pazza, amici miei!
Lasciatemi con lei, forse si calmerà!

Don Giovanni: *(trying to draw Elvira
away)* My friends, this poor young woman
is crazy! Leave her with me, and perhaps I
can calm her down!

Donna Elvira:
Ah! Non credete al perfido!

Donna Elvira:
Don't believe this perfidious man!

Don Giovanni:
È pazza, non badate!

Don Giovanni:
She's crazy, don't listen to her!

Donna Elvira:
Restate ancor, restate!

Donna Elvira:
Stay, stay!

Donna Anna e Don Ottavio:
A chi si crederà?

Donna Anna and Don Octavio:
Who should we believe?

Donna Anna, Don Ottavio, Don Giovanni:
Certo moto d'ignoto tormento
dentro l'alma girare mi sento;
Che mi dice, per quell'infelice.
Cento cose che intender non sa!

Donna Anna, Don Octavio, Don Giovanni:
I have a mysterious feeling
turning in my soul;
it tells me that she is an unhappy woman.
So many impossible things to understand!

Donna Elvira:
Sdegno, rabbia, dispetto, spavento.
Dentro l'alma girare mi sento,
che mi dice, di quel traditore.
Cento cose che intender non sa!

Donna Elvira:
I am fearful, scornful and angry
I have a mysterious feeling turning in my
soul; it tells me about this traitor.
So many impossible things to understand!

Don Ottavio:
(Io di qua non vado via se non so com'è
l'affar!)

Don Octavio:
(I will not leave from here until I learn the
truth of this mystery!)

Donna Anna:
Non ha l'aria di pazzia il suo tratto, il suo
parlar.

Donna Anna:
(She doesn't look or sound crazy to me.)

Don Giovanni:
(Se m'en vado, si potria qualche cosa
sospettar.)

Don Giovanni:
(If I go now, they'll become suspicious.)

Donna Elvira:
Da quel ceffo si dovria la ner'alma giudicar.

Donna Elvira: *(to Anna and Octavio)*
The dark soul of that beast should be judged.

Don Ottavio:
Dunque quella?

Don Octavio: *(to Don Giovanni)*
What does she say?

Don Giovanni:
È pazzarella!

Don Giovanni:
She's a little crazy!

Donna Anna:
Dunque quegli?

Donna Anna: *(to Elvira)*
And what do you say?

Donna Elvira:
È un traditore.

Donna Elvira:
He is a traitor.

Don Giovanni:
Infelice!

Don Giovanni:
Unhappy woman!

Donna Elvira:
Mentitore!

Donna Elvira:
Liar!

Donna Anna e Don Ottavio:
Incomincio a dubitar.

Donna Anna and Don Octavio: *doubt!*
I'm beginning to have doubts.

Don Giovanni:
Zitto, zitto, che la gente
si raduna a noi d'intorno;
siate un poco più prudente,
vi farete criticar.

Don Giovanni: *(aside to Elvira)*
Quiet, people are coming
and gathering all around,
be a little more prudent,
or else you'll be criticized.

Donna Elvira:
Non sperarlo, o scellerato,
ho perduta la prudenza;
le tue colpe ed il mio stato
voglio a tutti palesar.

Donna Elvira: *(loudly to Don Giovanni)*
Don't count on it, you scoundrel,
I have lost prudence;
I want to reveal to everyone
your sins and my sad fate.

Donna Anna e Don Ottavio:
Quegli accenti sì sommessi,
quel cangiarsi di colore,
son indizi troppo espressi.
Che mi fan determinar.

Donna Anna and Don Octavio:
He's altered his manner,
and his pallor has changed.
His expression makes me
see the truth.

Don Giovanni leads Elvira away, and then returns alone.

Don Giovanni:
Povera sventurata!
I passi suoi voglio seguir; non voglio che
faccia un precipizio.

Don Giovanni:
Poor woman!
I must follow her because I don't want her
to do something desperate.

Perdonate, bellissima Donn'Anna!
Se servirvi poss'io, in mia casa v'aspetto.
Amici, addio!

Forgive me, fair Donna Anna;
if I can serve you, I await you at my home.
Friends, farewell!

Don Giovanni departs hastily.

Donna Anna:
Don Ottavio! Son morta!

Donna Anna: *(in extreme agitation)*
Don Octavio! I'm petrified!

Don Ottavio:
Cosa è stato?

Don Octavio:
What is it?

Donna Anna:
Per pietà, soccorretemi!

Donna Anna:
For pity's sake, help me!

Don Ottavio:
Mio bene, fate coraggio!

Don Octavio:
My love, have courage!

Donna Anna:
Oh Dei! Quegli è il carnefice del padre mio!

Donna Anna:
Oh gods! He is the murderer of my father!

Don Ottavio:
Che dite?

Don Octavio:
What are you saying?

Donna Anna:
Non dubitate più. Gli ultimi accenti che
l'empio proferì, tutta la voce richiamar nel
cor mio di quell'indegno che nel mio
appartamento.

Donna Anna:
I know for sure. The intonation of his voice
reminds me of that contemptible villain who
barged into my apartment.

Don Ottavio:
O ciel! Possibile che sotto il sacro manto
d'amicizia ma come fu, narratemi lo strano
avvenimento.

Don Octavio:
Heavens! Can this be possible under the
sacred guise of friendship? But tell me what
happened.

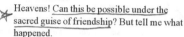

Donna Anna:
Era già alquanto avanzata la notte,
quando nelle mie stanze, ove soletta
mi trovai per sventura, entrar io vidi,
in un mantello avvolto, un uom che al
primo istante avea preso per voi.
Ma riconobbi poi che un inganno era il mio!

Donna Anna: *(extremely emotional)*
It was already late at night,
when I was alone in my rooms.
I saw someone enter, wrapped in a cloak,
a man, who at first I took for you.
But then I realized that I'd made a mistake!

Don Ottavio:
Stelle! Seguite!

Don Octavio: *(agitated)*
The wretch! Continue!

Donna Anna:
Tacito a me s'appresa e mi vuole
abbracciar;
sciogliermi cerco, ei più mi stringe;
io grido; non viene alcun:
con una mano cerca d'impedire la voce,
e coll'altra m'afferra stretta così,
che già mi credo vinta.

Donna Anna:
He approached me silently and then wanted
to kiss me.
I tried to free myself and shouted, but no
one came.
He covered my mouth with one hand,
and with the other grasped me so forcibly,
that I thought I was finished.

Don Ottavio:
Perfido! Alfin?

Don Octavio:
That villain! And then?

Donna Anna:
Alfine il duol, l'orrore dell'infame attentato
accrebbe sì la lena mia, che a forza di
svincolarmi, torcermi e piegarmi, da lui mi
sciolsi!

Donna Anna:
Finally my grief and despair strengthened
me against this infamous creature. After
struggling, twisting and turning, I freed
myself and escaped from him.

Don Ottavio:
Ohimè! Respiro!

Don Octavio:
I can breathe again!

Donna Anna:
Allora rinforzo i stridi miei, chiamo
soccorso; fugge il fellon;

Donna Anna:
Then I called for help, screaming louder as
the villain fled.

arditamente il seguo fin nella strada per fermarlo,
e sono assalitrice ed assalita:
il padre v'accorre, vuol conoscerlo e l'indegno
che del povero vecchio era più forte,
compiè il misfatto suo col dargli morte!

I boldly followed him into the street to stop him; as such, I became the assailant who was once the assailed.
My father ran to my aid and wanted to find out who it was.
But the old man was weaker than his foe; he was overpowered and met his doom!

Andante
DONNA ANNA

Or sai chi l'o - no - re ra - pi - re a me vol - se,

Or sai chi l'onore
aprire a me volse,
chi fu il traditore
che il padre mi tolse.
Vendetta ti chieggo,
la chiede il tuo cor!

I now know who it was who
tried to steal my honor,
and who the traitor was
who took my father from me.
It is vengeance I ask.
And your heart asks it too!

Rammenta la piaga
del misero seno,
rimira di sangue.
coperto il terreno.
Se l'ira in te langue
d'un giusto furor.

Remember the wound
in his poor breast,
and remember his blood
covering the ground,
if your anguish for a just revenge
should diminish.

Donna Anna departs.

Don Ottavio:
Come mai creder deggio,
di sì nero delitto capace un cavaliere!
Ah! Di scoprire il vero ogni mezzo si cerchi.
Io sento in petto
e di sposo e d'amico il dover che mi parla:
disingannarla voglio, o vendicarla!

Don Octavio:
How can one believe that this cavalier was capable of such a terrible crime!
Ah! I will use every means to discover the truth. I feel my heart speaking to me like her husband and friend. I wish to free her from deception and avenge her!

DON OTTAVIO

Dal-la sua pa - ce la mia di - pen - de,

Dalla sua pace la mia dipende;
quel che a lei piace vita mi rende,
quel che le incresce morte mi dà.
S'ella sospira, sospiro anch'io;
è mia quell'ira, quel pianto è mio;
e non ho bene, s'ella non l'ha!

My peace depends on her peace.
Whatever pleases her gives me joy,
what displeases her brings me death.
If she sighs, I also sigh,
because her anger is mine, and her tears are mine. I am not content if she is not content!

Don Octavio exits.

Leporello enters from the tavern, Don Giovanni from his palace.

Leporello:
Io deggio ad ogni patto per sempre
abbandonar questo bel matto.
Eccolo qui: guardate con qual indifferenza
se ne viene!

Leporello:
Whatever the consequence may be, I must
leave this mad rake forever.
Here he comes. Look at his indifferent air!

Don Giovanni:
Oh, Leporello mio! Va tutto bene?

Don Giovanni:
My Leporello! Does all go well?

Leporello:
Don Giovannino mio! Va tutto male!

Leporello:
My little Don Giovanni! All goes badly!

Don Giovanni:
Come va tutto male?

Don Giovanni:
Why badly?

Leporello:
Vado a casa, come voi m'ordinaste, con
tutta quella gente.

Leporello:
As you ordered me, I went to the house
with all those people.

Don Giovanni:
Bravo!

Don Giovanni:
Very good!

Leporello:
A forza di chiacchiere, di vezzi e di bugie,
ch'ho imparato sì bene a star con voi, cerco
d'intrattenerli.

Leporello:
I used lots of chatter and the usual
deceptions that I have learned so well
from you in my attempt to keep them there.

Don Giovanni:
Bravo!

Don Giovanni:
Very good!

Leporello:
Dico mille cose a Masetto per placarlo, per
trargli dal pensier la gelosia.

Leporello:
I said a thousand things to Masetto to pacify
him and erase any of his jealous thoughts.

Don Giovanni:
Bravo! In coscienza mia!

Don Giovanni:
Very good! A conscience like mine!

Leporello:
Faccio che bevano e gli uomini e le donne;
son già mezzo ubbriachi, altri canta, altri
scherza, altri seguita a ber. In sul più bello,
chi credete che capiti?

Leporello:
I had the men and women drinking; they
were already half drunk. Some were
singing, some joking, and others continued
to drink. Just as all was going well, who do
you think arrived?

Don Giovanni:
Zerlina!.

Don Giovanni:
Zerlina!

Leporello:
Bravo! E con lei chi viene?

Don Giovanni:
Donna Elvira!

Leporello:
Bravo! E disse di voi?

Don Giovanni:
Tutto quel mal che in bocca le venìa.

Leporello:
Bravo, in coscienza mia!

Don Giovanni:
E tu, cosa facesti?

Leporello:
Tacqui.

Don Giovanni:
Ed ella?

Leporello:
Seguì a gridar.

Don Giovanni:
E tu?

Leporello:
Quando mi parve che già fosse sfogata,
dolcemente fuor dell'orto la trassì, e con
bell'arte chiusa la porta a chiave io di là mi
cavai, e sulla via soletta la lasciai.

Don Giovanni:
Bravo! Bravo, arci bravo!
L'affar non può andar meglio.
Incominciasti, io saprò terminar.
Troppo mi premono queste contadinotte;
le voglio divertir finchè vien notte.

Leporello:
Right! And who do you think was with her?

Don Giovanni:
Donna Elvira!

Leporello:
Right! Did she tell you?

Don Giovanni:
All the evil she could imagine came from
her lips!

Leporello:
True, upon my word!

Don Giovanni:
And what did you do?

Leporello:
Nothing.

Don Giovanni:
And she?

Leporello:
Continued to shout.

Don Giovanni:
And you?

Leporello:
When she appeared to be exhausted,
I gently led her out of the garden, and then
adroitly closed the door, locked it and rode
off. I left her standing alone in the street.

Don Giovanni:
Superb! Superb, absolutely perfect! The
affair could not have gone better. What you
began, I will finish. These pretty country
girls bewitch me. I want to amuse them
until nightfall.

Presto
DON GIOVANNI

Finch' han dal vi - no cal - da la te - sta,
While they're cheerful from wine

u - na gran fe - sta fa pre - pa - rar!
go and prepare a feast!

Finch'han dal vino calda la testa
una gran festa fa preparar!
Se trovi in piazza qualche ragazza,
teco ancor quella cerca menar.

Senza alcun ordine la danza sia,
chi il minuetto, chi la follia,
chi l'alemanna farai ballar!

Ed io frattanto dall'altro canto
con questa e quella vo' amoreggiar.
Ah! La mia lista doman mattina
d'una decina devi aumentar!

While they're cheerful from wine
go and prepare a feast!
If you find some girl in the plaza,
bring her with you.

Without further ado, get the dance going.
Make them dance, a minuet, a frolic,
or the allemande!

And I'll be among them,
making love with this one or that one.
Tomorrow morning,
my list must increase by a dozen!   *ASS!*

Leporello goes into the tavern to fetch the peasants. Don Giovanni rushes into his palace.

ACT I - Scene 4

A garden. On one side, Don Giovanni's palace; on the other, a pavilion.

Zerlina:
Masetto, senti un po'! Masetto, dico!

Masetto:
Non mi toccar!

Zerlina:
Perchè?

Masetto:
Perchè mi chiedi? Perfida! Il tocco
sopportar dovrei d'una mano infedele?

Zerlina:
Ah no, taci, crudele, io non merito da te tal
trattamento.

Zerlina:
Masetto, listen a moment to what I have to
say!

Masetto:
Don't touch me!

Zerlina:
Why?

Masetto:
You don't know why? Betrayer! Must I
touch your unfaithful hand?

Zerlina:
Oh no. You're cruel. I don't deserve such
treatment.

Masetto:
Come? Ed hai l'ardimento di scusarti?
Star solo con un uom, abbandonarmi il dì
delle mie nozze!
Porre in fronte a un villano d'onore questa
marca d'infamia!
Ah, se non fosse, se non fosse lo scandalo,
vorrei...

Masetto:
Why? Do you have the audacity to make
excuses? You were alone with a man and
abandoned me on our wedding day!
To do this with such a villain is a mark of
disgrace!
And if it were not because I fear a scandal,
I would…

Zerlina:
Ma se colpa io non ho, ma se da lui
ingannata rimasi; e poi, che temi?
Tranquillati, mia vita; non mi toccò la punta
della dita.
Non me lo credi? Ingrato!
Vien qui, sfogati, ammazzami, fa tutto di
me quel che ti piace, ma poi, Masetto mio,
ma poi fa pace.

Zerlina:
He tried to deceive me, but I did nothing
wrong. So what do you fear?
Be calm, he didn't touch the tip of my
finger. Don't you believe me?
You're so ungrateful! Come here!
Vent your anger, kill me, do what you want
to me, but then, my dear Masetto, but then
let's make peace.

Andante grazioso
ZERLINA

Bat - ti   bat-ti o   bel   Ma-set - to,   la   tua   po - ve -ra   Zer - li - na,

Batti, batti, o bel Masetto,
la tua povera Zerlina;
Starò qui come agnellina
le tue botte ad aspettar.
Lascerò straziarmi il crine,
lascerò cavarmi gli occhi, e le care tue
manine lieta poi saprò baciar.

Beat me, beat me, dear Masetto,
beat your poor Zerlina.
I'll be like a patient lamb
and await your flogging.
I'll let you tear out my hair, I'll let you dig
out my eyes, and then I'll happily kiss those
dear hands of yours.

Ah, lo vedo, non hai core!
Pace, pace, o vita mia,
in contento ed allegria
notte e dì vogliam passar,
Sì, notte e dì vogliam passar.

Oh, I see you haven't the heart!
Peace, peace, my love,
Let's spend night and day
in peace and contentment Yes, in peace and
contentment.

Masetto:
Guarda un po' come seppe questa strega
sedurmi! Siamo pure i deboli di testa!

Masetto:
Look how this enchantress has seduced me!
We men must all have weak minds!

Don Giovanni:
Sia preparato tutto a una gran festa.

Don Giovanni: *(from inside)*
Prepare a grand feast for everyone.

Zerlina:
Ah Masetto, Masetto, odi la voce del monsù
cavaliere!

Zerlina: *(frightened)*
Oh, Masetto, Masetto, it's the voice of the
cavalier!

Masetto:
Ebben, che c'è?

Masetto:
Well, what of that?

Zerlina:
Verrà!

Zerlina:
He'll be coming here!

Masetto:
Lascia che venga.

Masetto:
Let him come.

Zerlina:
Ah, se vi fosse un buco da fuggir!

Zerlina:
Oh, if only there was a place to hide from him!

Masetto:
Di cosa temi?
Perché diventi pallida?
Ah, capisco! Capisco, bricconcella,
hai timor ch'io comprenda com'è tra voi
passata la faccenda.

Masetto:
What are you afraid of?
Why do you turn pale?
Ah, I understand! I understand, you little
cheat, you're afraid that I'll find out what
took place between the both of you.

Presto, presto, pria ch'ei venga,
por mi vo' da qualche lato;
c'è una nicchia qui celato, cheto cheto mi
vo' star.

Quickly, quickly, before he comes. I'll move
aside.
There's a nook. I'll stay there and hide
quietly.

Zerlina:
Senti, senti, dove vai? Ah, non t'asconder, o
Masetto! Se ti trova, poveretto, tu non sai
quel che può far.

Zerlina:
Listen, listen, where are you going?
Masetto, don't hide! If he finds you, my poor
fellow, you don't know what he might do.

Masetto:
Faccia, dica quel che vuole.

Masetto:
Let him say or do what he wishes.

Zerlina:
Ah, non giovan le parole!

Zerlina:
Words are just useless!

Masetto:
Parla forte, e qui t'arresta!

Masetto;
Speak louder so I can hear you!

Zerlina:
Che capriccio hai nella testa?

Zerlina:
What nonsense do you have in your mind?

Masetto:(
Capirò se m'è fedele, e in qual modo andò
l'affar!)

Masetto:
(I will learn whether she is faithful, and just
how far their intrigue went!)

Zerlina:
(Quell'ingrato, quel crudele, oggi vuol
precipitar.)

Zerlina:
(How cruel and ungrateful! He's looking
for trouble today.)

Masetto hides in the arbor as Don Giovanni arrives.

Don Giovanni:
Sù! Svegliatevi da bravi!
Sù! Coraggio, o buona gente!
Vogliam star allegramente,
vogliam ridere e scherzar.

Alla stanza, della danza
conducete tutti quanti,
ed a tutti in abbondanza
gran rifreschi fate dar!

Coro:
Sù! Svegliatevi da bravi!

Don Giovanni: *(to the peasants)*
Come on! Get up and enjoy yourselves!
Come! Be hearty good people!
Let's be happy!
Let's laugh and play!

(to the servants)
Take all of them to the hall
for dancing,
and give them all
plenty of great refreshments!

Chorus of peasants:
Come on! Get up and enjoy yourselves!

After the peasants leave, Zerlina tries to hide herself among the trees.

Zerlina:
Tra quest'arbori celata, si può dar che non mi veda.

Zerlina:
Perhaps he won't see me if I am concealed among these trees.

Don Giovanni:
Zerlinetta, mia garbata, t'ho già visto, non scappar!

Don Giovanni:
My sweet Zerlina, I now see you, and you cannot escape!

Zerlina:
Ah lasciatemi andar via!

Zerlina:
Let me go away!

Don Giovanni:
No, no, resta, gioia mia!

Don Giovanni:
No, stay, my angel!

Zerlina:
Se pietade avete in core!

Zerlina:
If you have one bit of pity in your heart!

Don Giovanni:
Sì, ben mio! Son tutto amore. Vieni un poco, in questo loco fortunata io ti vo' far!

Don Giovanni:
Yes, my dearest! I'm all love. Come with me, it will be worthwhile for you!

Zerlina:
(Ah, s'ei vede il sposo mio, so ben io quel che può far!)

Zerlina:
(Oh, if my jealous fiancé sees him, I know well what he could do!)

Don Giovanni discovers the hiding Masetto.

Don Giovanni:
Masetto?

Don Giovanni:
Masetto?

Masetto:
Sì, Masetto!

Masetto:
Yes, Masetto!

Don Giovanni:
E chiuso là, perchè? La bella tua Zerlina
non può, la poverina, più star senza di te.

Don Giovanni:
And why are you hiding there? Your pretty
Zerlina, poor thing, can no longer be
without you.

Masetto:
Capisco, sì signore.

Masetto: *(with irony)*
I understand, my lord.

Don Giovanni:
Adesso fate core. I suonatori udite? Venite
ormai con me!

Don Giovanni:
Come, be strong. Do you hear the
musicians? Now come with me!

Zerlina e Masetto:
Sì, sì, facciamo core, ad a ballar cogli altri.
Andiamo tutti tre!

Zerlina and Masetto:
Yes, yes, let's all capture the spirit, and dance
with the others. Let's all three go together!

Don Giovanni, Zerlina and Masetto leave for the ball.

*As evening descends. Don Octavio, Donna Anna and Donna Elvira arrive;
all are masked.*

Donna Elvira:
Bisogna aver coraggio, o cari amici miei,
e i suoi misfatti rei scoprir potremo allor.

Donna Elvira:
We must be courageous, my dear friends,
and then we can uncover his wicked deeds.

Don Ottavio:
L'amica dice bene, coraggio aver conviene;
Discaccia, o vita mia, l'affanno ed il timor!

Don Octavio: *(to Donna Anna).*
Our friend speaks wisely-, we must be
righteous. Oh my dearest, your fear and
terror will soon end!

Donna Anna:
Il passo è periglioso, può nascer qualche
imbroglio.
Temo pel caro sposo,
e per voi temo ancor!

Donna Anna:
This action is dangerous, and can lead to a
squabble.
I fear for my beloved fiancé,
(to Donna Elvira) and for you as well!

Leporello points out the masqueraders to Don Giovanni.

Leporello:
Signor, guardate un poco, che maschere
galanti!

Leporello:
Sir, take a moment and look at the gallant
masqueraders! ~appearance!

Don Giovanni:
Falle passar avanti, di' che ci fanno onor!

Don Giovanni:
Invite them in, and tell them we would be
honored!

**Donna Anna, Donna Elvira e Don
Ottavio:**
(Al volto ed alla voce si scopre il traditore!)

**Donna Anna, Donna Elvira and Don
Octavio:**
(The traitor reveals himself by his bearing
and his voice!)

Leporello:
Zì, zì! Signore maschere!

Leporello:
Psst, psst! Noble masqueraders!

Donna Anna e Donna Elvira:
Via, rispondete.

Donna Anna, Donna Elvira: *(to Octavio)*
Go, you respond to him.

Leporello:
Signore maschere!

Leporello:
Noble masqueraders!

Don Ottavio:
Cosa chiedete?

Don Octavio:
What are you asking for?

Leporello:
Al ballo, se vi piace, v'invita il mio signor.

Leporello:
My lord invites you, if you would, to join the ball.

Don Ottavio:
Grazie di tanto onore!
Andiam, compagne belle.

Don Octavio:
Thank you for such an honor!
Let's go, beautiful companions.

Leporello:
(L'amico anche su quelle prova farà
d'amor!)

Leporello:
(My lord will quickly try to make love to
the women!)

Leporello enters the palace.

Donna Anna e Don Ottavio:
Protegga il giusto cielo il zelo del mio cor!

Donna Anna and Don Octavio:
May the just heavens protect the fierceness
in my heart!

Donna Elvira:
Vendichi il giusto cielo il mio tradito amor!

Donna Elvira:
May the just heavens avenge my betrayed
love!

The three masqueraders enter the palace.

ACT I - Scene 5

The brilliantly illuminated ballroom of Don Giovanni's palace.

Don Giovanni:
Riposate, vezzose ragazze.

Don Giovanni:
(ushering some young girls to seats)
Pretty girls, rest from your dancing.

Leporello:
Rinfrescatevi, bei giovinotti!

Leporello:
Good men, some refreshments!

Don Giovanni e Leporello:
Tornerete a far presto le pazze, tornerete a
scherzar e ballar!

Don Giovanni and Leporello:
You'll soon be returning to your passions of
playing and dancing!

Don Giovanni:
Ehi! Caffè!

Don Giovanni:
Hey! Some coffee!

Leporello:
Cioccolata!

Leporello:
Some chocolate!

Masetto:
Ah, Zerlina, giudizio!

Masetto: *(anxiously holding Zerlina)*
Zerlina, be prudent!

Don Giovanni:
Sorbetti!

Don Giovanni:
Sherbet!

Leporello:
Confetti!

Leporello:
Some sweets!

Masetto:
Ah, Zerlina, giudizio!

Masetto:
Zerlina, be prudent!

Zerlina e Masetto:
(Troppo dolce comincia la scena; in amaro
potrìa terminar!)

Zerlina and Masetto:
(The scene begins so sweetly, but may end
bitterly!)

Don Giovanni:
Sei pur vaga, brillante Zerlina!

Don Giovanni:
Lovely Zerlina, you are indeed charming!

Zerlina:
Sua bontà!

Zerlina:
Your lordship is very polite!

Masetto:
(La briccona fa festa!)

Masetto: *(aside furiously).*
(The rascal is enjoying herself!)

Leporello:
Sei pur cara, Gionnotta, Sandrina.

Leporello: *(amongst the girls)*
How pretty you are, Giannotta, Sandrina!

Masetto:
(Tocca pur, che ti cada la testa!)

Masetto:
(Touch her and your head will fall!)

Zerlina:
(Quel Masetto mi par stralunato, brutto,
brutto si fa quest'affar!)

Zerlina: *(looking at Masetto)*
(That Masetto has gone mad; he's in an
awful predicament!)

Don Giovanni e Leporello:
(Quel Masetto mi par stralunato,
qui bisogna cervello adoprar.)

Don Giovanni and Leporello:
(That Masetto seems a little crazy.
I must use all my skill to win her.)

The masqueraders enter the ballroom.

Leporello:
Venite pur avanti, vezzose mascherette!

Leporello:
Come forward, charming masqueraders!

Don Giovanni:
È aperto a tutti quanti.
Viva la libertà!

Don Giovanni:
My house is open to everyone.
Long live liberty!

Donna Anna, Donna Elvira e Don Ottavio:
Siam grati a tanti segni di generosità!

Donna Anna, Donna Elvira and Don Octavio:
We are grateful for those gestures of hospitality!

Tutti:
Viva la libertà!

All:
Long live liberty!

Don Giovanni:
Ricominciate il suono!
Tu accoppia i ballerini!

Don Giovanni:
Go on with the music!
(to Leporello) You pair the dancers!

Don Giovanni addresses the masqueraders.

Da bravi, via ballate!

Good people, come and dance!

Don Giovanni begins to dance with Zerlina.

Donna Elvira:

(Quella è la contadina.)

Donna Elvira:
(to Donna Anna pointing out Zerlina)
(That is the country girl.)

Donna Anna:
(Io moro!)

Donna Anna: *(to Don Octavio)*
(I feel like I am dying!)

Don Ottavio:
(Simulate!)

Don Octavio: *(to Donna Anna)*
(Hide your feelings!)

Don Giovanni e Leporello:
Va bene in verità!

Don Giovanni and Leporello:
All is going well!

Masetto:
Va bene in verità!

Masetto: *(ironically)*
Yes, everything is going well!

Don Giovanni:
A bada tien Masetto.

Don Giovanni: *(to Leporello)*
Take good care of Masetto.

Leporello:
Non balli, poveretto! Vien quà, Masetto caro, facciam quel ch'altri fa.

Leporello: *(to Masetto)*
You're not dancing! Come here, my friend Masetto, and let us do as the others.

Don Giovanni:
Il tuo compagno io sono. Zerlina vien pur qua!

Leporello:
Eh, balla, amico mio!

Masetto:
No!

Leporello:
Sì! Caro Masetto!

Masetto:
No, no, ballar non voglio!

Donna Anna:
Resister non poss'io!

Donna Elvira e Don Ottavio:
Fingete per pietà!

Don Giovanni: (to *Zerlina)*
I am your partner. Zerlina come with me!
(Leporello dances with Masetto)

Leporello:
Hey, dance my friend!

Masetto:
No!

Leporello:
Yes! Dear Masetto!

Masetto:
No, no, I don't want to dance!

Donna Anna:
I can no longer endure!

Donna Elvira and Don Octavio:
Pretend, for pity's sake!

Don Giovanni places his arm about Zerlina's waist
and draws her toward a door.

Don Giovanni:
Vieni con me, vita mia!

Masetto:
Lasciami! Ah no! Zerlina!

Zerlina:
Oh Numi! Son tradita!

Don Giovanni:
Come with me, my love!

Masetto: *(to Leporello)*
Leave me alone! Oh no! Zerlina!

Zerlina:
Oh, Heavens I'm betrayed!

Don Giovanni forces Zerlina into the room.

Leporello:
Qui nasce una ruina.

Donna Anna, Donna Elvira e Don Ottavio:
L'iniquo da se stesso nel laccio se ne va!

Zerlina:
Gente, aiuto! Aiuto! Gente!

Leporello:
Another disaster is being born.

Donna Anna, Donna Elvira and Don Octavio:
The vile intriguer will be caught in his own trap!

Zerlina: *(from within the room)*
Help me! Someone help me!

**Donna Anna, Donna Elvira e Don
Ottavio:**
Soccorriamo l'innocente!

**Donna Anna, Donna Elvira e Don
Octavio:**
Let's save the innocent girl!

Masetto:
Ah, Zerlina!

Masetto:
Oh, Zerlina!

Zerlina:
Scellerato!

Zerlina: *(from within)*
Evil man!

**Donna Anna, Donna Elvira e Don
Ottavio:**
Ora grida da quel lato!
Ah gettiamo giù la porta!

**Donna Anna, Donna Elvira and Don
Octavio:**
The shout comes from that side!
Let's break down the door!

Zerlina:
Soccorretemi! O son morta!

Zerlina: *(from within)*
Save me, or I'll die!

**Donna Anna, Donna Elvira, Don
Ottavio e Masetto:**
Siam qui noi per tua difesa!

**Donna Anna, Donna Elvira and Don
Octavio:**
We're here to defend you!

They break open the door. Don Giovanni emerges holding Leporello by the arm.

Don Giovanni:
Ecco il birbo che t'ha offesa! Ma da me la
pena avrà! Mori, iniquo!

Don Giovanni:
Here is the culprit who offended you! But
my hand shall punish him! Die, criminal!

Leporello:
Ah, cosa fate?

Leporello:
What are you doing?

Don Giovanni:
Mori, dico!

Don Giovanni:
Die, criminal!

Don Ottavio:

Nol sperate.

Don Octavio:
(holding a pistol to Giovanni)
Don't have hope that you can escape.

**Donna Anna, Donna Elvira e Don
Ottavio:**
(L'empio crede con tal frode di nasconder
l'empietà!)

**Donna Anna, Donna Elvira and Don
Octavio:** *(all unmask)*
(The villain thinks he can hide his
wickedness from us!)

Don Giovanni:
Donna Elvira?

Don Giovanni:
Donna Elvira?

Donna Elvira:
Sì, malvagio!

Donna Elvira:
Yes, you false one!

Don Giovanni:
Don Ottavio?

Don Giovanni:
Don Octavio?

Don Ottavio:
Sì, signore!

Don Octavio:
Yes, Signor!

Don Giovanni:
Ah, credete.

Don Giovanni:
Unbelievable.

Donna Anna:
Traditore!

Donna Anna:
You traitor!

Donna Anna, Donna Elvira e Don Ottavio:
Traditore! Traditore! Tutto già si sa!

Donna Anna, Donna Elvira and Don Octavio:
Traitor! Traitor! Everything is now known!

They approach Don Giovanni threateningly.

Trema, trema, o scellerato!

Tremble, tremble, scoundrel!

Zerlina:
Saprà tosto il mondo intero
il misfatto orrendo e nero
la tua fiera crudeltà!

Zerlina:
My head is confused
from your dark and horrible deeds
and your fierce cruelty!

Tutti:
Odi il tuon della vendetta,
che ti fischia intorno intorno;
Sul tuo capo in questo giorno
il suo fulmine cadrà!

All: *(except Giovanni and Leporello)*
Hear the thunder of vengeance,
that roars all around.
On this day, a thunderbolt
will fall on his head!

Don Giovanni e Leporello:
È confusa la mia testa!
Non sa più quel ch'ei si faccia
È un orribile tempesta minacciando,
o Dio, lo va!

Don Giovanni and Leporello:
My head is confused!
I do not know what I should do.
It is a horrible menacing storm
that God has wrought!

Ma non manca in lui coraggio,
non si perde o si confonde.
Se cadesse ancora il mondo,
nulla mai temer lo fa!

But my courage doesn't fail me,
I'm not lost or confused.
If the world might yet fall apart,
there is nothing I fear!

Don Giovanni seizes Leporello. Both push their way through the crowd and escape.

$$\boxed{\text{ACT II - Scene 1}}$$

Don Giovanni and Leporello stand before the balcony of Donna Elvira's house.

Don Giovanni:
Eh via, buffone, non mi seccar!

Don Giovanni:
Come on buffoon, don't annoy me!

Leporello:
No, no, padrone, non vo'restar.

Leporello:
No, master, I want to leave you.

Don Giovanni:
Sentimi, amico.

Don Giovanni:
Listen to me, my friend.

Leporello:
Vo'andar, vi dico!

Leporello:
I tell you that I'm leaving!

Don Giovanni:
Ma che ti ho fatto che vuoi lasciarmi?

Don Giovanni:
What have I done that makes you want
to leave me?

Leporello:
O niente affatto!
Quasi ammazzarmi!

Leporello:
Of course nothing important!
It's just that you almost had me killed!

Don Giovanni:
Va, che sei matto, fu per burlar

Don Giovanni:
Go away. You're crazy. It was a joke.

Leporello:
Ed io non burlo, ma voglio andar!

Leporello:
I'm not joking, I want to leave you!

Don Giovanni:

Leporello!

Don Giovanni:
(Don Giovanni tries to detain Leporello)
Leporello!

Leporello:
Signore!

Leporello:
Sir!

Don Giovanni:
Vien qui, facciamo pace, prendi!

Don Giovanni: *(gives him a purse)*
Here, let's make peace. Take this!

Leporello:
Cosa?

Leporello:
How much?

Don Giovanni::
Quattro doppie.

Don Giovanni:
Four gold pieces.

Leporello:
Oh, sentite: per questa volta la ceremonia
accetto; ma non vi ci avvezzate;
non credete di sedurre i miei pari, come le
donne, a forza di danari.

Leporello: *(counting the money)*
O.K. Listen, I'll accept it just this once,
but don't make it a habit. Don't think that
you can seduce me with the power of money
the way you do the women.

Don Giovanni:
Non parliam più di ciò!
Ti basta l'animo di far quel ch'io ti dico?

Don Giovanni:
Let's not talk about it anymore!
Do you have the courage to do what
I'm about to tell you?

Leporello:
Purchè lasciam le donne.

Leporello:
Provided we give up women.

Don Giovanni:
Lasciar le donne? Pazzo!
Sai ch'elle per me son necessarie più del pan
che mangio,
più dell'aria che spiro!

Don Giovanni:
Give up women? You're mad!
You know that they're more necessary
to me than the bread I eat, or the air I
breathe!

Leporello:
E avete core d'ingannarle poi tutte?

Leporello:
And why do you have the heart to
deceive all of them?

Don Giovanni:
È tutto amore! Chi a una sola è fedele, verso
l'altre è crudele:
io che in me sento sì esteso sentimento,
vo' bene a tutte quante.
Le donne poiché calcolar non sanno,
il mio buon natural chiamano inganno.

Don Giovanni:
It is all for love! A man who is faithful to
one, is cruel to all the others.
I, who has within me such immense
feelings, I want to love them all.
But, the women misinterpret my good
intentions and consider them deceptions.

Leporello:
Non ho veduto mai naturale più vasto, e più
benigno.
Orsù, cosa vorreste?

Leporello:
I have never seen such grand
benevolence, and such a good nature.
Now, what do you want me to do?

Don Giovanni:
Odi! Vedesti tu la cameriera di Donna
Elvira?

Don Giovanni:
Listen! Have you seen Donna Elvira's
maid?

Leporello:
Io? No!

Leporello:
Me? No!

Don Giovanni:
Non hai veduto qualche cosa di bello, caro il
mio Leporello;
ora io con lei vo' tentar la mia sorte, ed ho
pensato, giacché siam verso sera, per

Don Giovanni:
Then my dear Leporello, you have
missed something lovely. Right now, I'm
going to try my luck with her, and I've
been thinking, since it's almost evening,

aguzzarle meglio l'appetito di presentarmi a lei col tuo vestito.

I'll arouse her appetite by presenting myself in your clothes.

Leporello:
E perchè non potreste presentarvi col vostro?

Leporello:
And why can't you present yourself in your own clothes?

Don Giovanni:
Han poco credito con genti di tal rango gli abiti signorili.

Don Giovanni:
With people like her, the dress of a noble would appear too fine.

(Don Giovanni takes off his cloak)

Sbrigati, via!

Be quick!

Leporello:
Signor, per più ragioni...

Leporello:
Sir, I've a suspicion....

Don Giovanni:
Finiscila! Non soffro opposizioni!

Don Giovanni:
Stop it! I can't stand opposition!

Don Giovanni and Leporello exchange cloaks and hats.

Donna Elvira:
Ah taci, ingiusto core!
Non palpitarmi in seno!
È un empio, e un traditore.
È colpa di aver pietà.

Donna Elvira: *(from her balcony)*
Be silent, inconsiderate heart!
Don't throb in my breast!
He's merciless, and he's a deceiver.
It's shameful to have pity for him.

Leporello:
(Zitto! Di Donna Elvira, Signor, la voce io sento!)

Leporello:
(Sssh! I hear Donna Elvira's voice!)

Don Giovanni:
(Cogliere io vo' il momento, tu fermati un po' là!)

Don Giovanni:
(I'll seize the opportunity! You stand over there!)

Don Giovanni stands behind Leporello and makes gestures with Leporello's arms.

Elvira, idolo mio!

Elvira, my idol!

Donna Elvira:
Non è costui l'ingrato?

Donna Elvira:
Is that the ingrate?

Don Giovanni:
Si, vita mia, son io, e chieggo carità.

Don Giovanni:
Yes, my dearest, it is I, and I ask for your forgiveness.

Donna Elvira:
(Numi, che strano affetto, mi si risveglia in petto!)

Donna Elvira:
(Gods, what strange emotion he arouses in my breast!)

Leporello:
(State a veder la pazza, che ancor gli crederà!)

Leporello:
(Look at that crazy woman! She still believes him!)

Don Giovanni:
Discendi, o gioia bella, vedrai che tu sei quella che adora l'alma mia pentito io sono già.

Don Giovanni:
Come down, my beautiful jewel, and you'll see that you are the one who my soul adores. I have already repented.

Donna Elvira:
No, non ti credo, o barbaro!

Donna Elvira:
I don't believe you, you barbarian!

Don Giovanni:
Ah credimi, o m'uccido!
Idolo mio, vien qua!

Don Giovanni:
Believe me, or I'll kill myself!
My idol, come here!

Leporello:
(Se seguitate, io rido!)

Leporello:
(If you continue, I'll burst out laughing!)

Donna Elvira:
(Dei, che cimento è questo!
Non so s'io vado o resto!
Ah proteggete voi la mia credulità!)

Donna Elvira:
(Gods, what agony this is!
I don't know whether to go or remain!
Gods, protect me from my uncertainty!)

Don Giovanni:
(Spero che cada presto!
Che bel colpetto è questo!
Più fertile talento del mio, no, non si dà!)

Don Giovanni:
(I think it worked well!
What an ingenious stroke this was!
A more fertile talent than mine doesn't exist!)

Leporello:
(Già quel mendace labbro torna a sedur costei, deh proteggete, o dei!
La sua credulità!)

Leporello:
(What a smooth deceiver he is!
I hope the gods protect her from her uncertainty!)

Elvira leaves the balcony

Don Giovanni:
Amore, che ti par?

Don Giovanni: *(happily)*
What do you think?

Leporello:
Mi par che abbiate un'anima di bronzo.

Leporello:
I think that you are heartless.

Don Giovanni:
Va là, che sei il gran gonzo!
Ascolta bene: quando costei qui viene,
tu corri ad abbracciarla, falle quattro carezze,
fingi la voce mia: poi con bell'arte cerca teco
condurla in altra parte.

Leporello:
Ma, Signor...

Don Giovanni:
Non più repliche!

Leporello:
Ma se poi mi conosce?

Don Giovanni:
Non ti conoscerà, se tu non vuoi.
Zitto: ell'apre, ehi giudizio!

Don Giovanni:
So be it. What a fool you are!
Now listen to me. When she comes out, run
and embrace her, give her four kisses, and
mimic my voice. Then use your ingenuity
and take her somewhere else.

Leporello:
But, sir...

Don Giovanni:
No more talk!

Leporello:
But what if she recognizes me?

Don Giovanni:
She won't recognize you, if you don't want her to.
Quiet! She's opening the door, so be smart!

Don Giovanni rushes off to the side, leaving Leporello alone.
Donna Elvira emerges from the house, and advances toward Leporello.

✱ appearance vs. reality!

Donna Elvira:
Eccomi a voi.

Don Giovanni:
(Veggiamo che farà.)

Leporello:
(Che bell'imbroglio!)

Donna Elvira:
Dunque creder potrò che i pianti miei abbian
vinto quel cor?
Dunque pentito l'amato Don Giovanni al
suo dovere all'amor mio ritorna?

Leporello:
Sì, carina!

Donna Elvira:
Crudele! Se sapeste quante lagrime e quanti
sospir voi mi costaste!

Leporello:
Io, vita mia?

Donna Elvira: *(to Leporello)*
I am here for you.

Don Giovanni: *(to Leporello)*
(Let's see what will happen.)

Leporello:
(What a beautiful predicament!)

Donna Elvira:
Could I ever have believed that my tears
have won your heart?
Has my beloved Don Giovanni repented,
and returned to me virtuous and faithful?

Leporello: *(imitating Don Giovanni's voice)*
Yes, beloved!

Donna Elvira:
You cruel man! If you only knew much I cried
and longed for you!

Leporello:
My beloved, for me?

Donna Elvira:
Voi.

Leporello:
Poverina! Quanto mi dispiace!

Donna Elvira:
Mi fuggirete più?

Leporello:
No, muso bello!

Donna Elvira:
Sarete sempre mio?

Leporello:
Sempre!

Donna Elvira:
Carissimo!

Leporello:
Carissima!
(La burla mi dà gusto.)

Donna Elvira:
Mio tesoro!

Leporello:
Mia Venere!

Donna Elvira:
Son per voi tutta foco.

Leporello:
Io tutto cenere.

Don Giovanni:
(Il birbo si riscalda.)

Donna Elvira:
E non m'ingannerete?

Leporello:
No, sicuro.

Donna Elvira:
Giuratelo.

Donna Elvira:
Yes, for you.

Leporello:
Poor lady! I'm so sorry for you!

Donna Elvira:
Will you ever leave me again?

Leporello:
No, my beautiful inspiration!

Donna Elvira:
Will you always be mine?

Leporello:
Always!

Donna Elvira:
My dearest!

Leporello:
My dearest!
(I'm really enjoying this game.)

Donna Elvira:
My treasure!

Leporello:
My Venus!

Donna Elvira: *(embracing him)*
I'm all aflame for you.

Leporello:
And I am all burned to ashes.

Don Giovanni:
(The rogue is warming up to it.)

Donna Elvira:
Will you ever deceive me again?

Leporello:
Certainly not.

Donna Elvira:
Swear it.

Leporello:
Lo giuro a questa mano, che bacio con
trasporto, e a que' bei lumi.

Leporello:
I swear it by this hand, my kiss for you,
and on your beautiful eyes.

Don Giovanni:
Ah, eh, ah, ah!
Sei morto.

Don Giovanni:
(pretending to thrash someone)
Ah, ha, you wretch, you're dead!

Donna Elvira e Leporello:
Oh numi!

Donna Elvira and Leporello:
Oh, heavens!

In fear, Donna Elvira and Leporello flee together.

Don Giovanni:
Ha, ha, ha! Par che la sorte mi secondi;
veggiamo! Le finestre son queste.
Ora cantiamo.

Don Giovanni:
Ha, ha, ha! It seems that luck is
with me! Let's see! These are the
windows. Now, we'll sing the serenade.

Don Giovanni serenades Donna Elvira's maid,
accompanying himself with the mandolin Leporello left behind.

Allegretto
DON GIOVANNI

Deh   vie - ni alla   fi - ne-stra,   o   mio   te - so - ro,

Deh, vieni alla finestra, o mio tesoro,
deh, vieni a consolar il pianto mio.
Se neghi a me di dar qualche ristoro,
davanti agli occhi tuoi morir vogl'io!

Come to the window, my treasure.
Come and console my tears.
If you refuse to give me some
solace, I wish to die before your eyes!

Tu ch'hai la bocca dolce più del miele,
Tu che il zucchero porti in mezzo al core!
Non esser, gioia mia, con me crudele!
Lasciati almen veder, mio bell'amore!

Your mouth is sweeter than honey!
You carry sweetness in your heart!
My treasure, don't be cruel to me!
My beautiful love let me at least see you!

Don Giovanni:
V'è gente alla finestra,
forse è dessa! Sst! Sst!

Don Giovanni:
There's someone at the window.
Perhaps it is she! Psst! Psst!

Masetto arrives, armed with a gun and pistol. Peasants follow him.

Masetto:
Non ci stanchiamo;
il cor mi dice che trovarlo dobbiam.

Masetto: *(to the peasants)*
Let's never give up. My intuition tells me
that we should find him here.

Don Giovanni:
(Qualcuno parla!)

Don Giovanni:
(Someone is speaking!)

Masetto:
Fermatevi; mi pare che alcuno qui si muova.

Masetto: *(to the peasants)*
Stop here! It seems to me that someone
moved.

Don Giovanni:

(Se non fallo, è Masetto!)

Don Giovanni:
(hiding himself with his cloak and hat)
(If I'm not mistaken, it's Masetto!)

Masetto:
Chi va là? Non risponde; animo,
schioppo al muso! Chi va là?

Masetto;
Who's there? No one answers.
Be courageous friends, and have your
muskets ready! Who's there?

Don Giovanni:
(Non è solo, ci vuol giudizio.)

Amici. (Non mi voglio scoprir.)
Sei tu, Masetto?

Don Giovanni:
(He's not alone. I better be careful.)
(imitating Leporello)
Friends. (I don't want them to recognize me.)
Masetto, is that you?

Masetto:
Appunto quello; e tu?

Masetto:
Precisely, and you?

Don Giovanni:
Non mi conosci? Il servo son io di Don
Giovanni.

Don Giovanni:
Don't you recognize me? I'm Don
Giovanni's servant.

Masetto:
Leporello! Servo di quell'indegno cavaliere!

Masetto:
Leporello! The servant of that
disreputable cavalier!

Don Giovanni:
Certo; di quel briccone!

Don Giovanni:
That's right, the servant of that rascal!

Masetto:
Di quell'uom senza onore: ah, dimmi un
poco dove possiam trovarlo? Lo cerco con
costor per trucidarlo!

Masetto;
Of that dishonorable man. Tell me,
where we can find him? We're all
looking to slaughter him!

Don Giovanni:
(Bagattelle!) Bravissimo, Masetto!
Anch'io con voi m'unisco, per fargliela a
quel birbo di padrone.
Ma udite un po' qual è la mia intenzione.

Don Giovanni:
(So that's all!) Great, Masetto!
I'll join you to help you catch my wicked
master. But listen a moment to what I
have in mind.

Metà di voi qua vadano,
e gli altri vadan là!
E pian pianin lo cerchino.
Lontan non fia di qua!

Half of you go this way,
and the rest go that way!
And we'll look for him very quietly.
He can't be far from here!

Se un uom e una ragazza	If you should see a man and a lady walk
passeggian per la piazza,	through the square,
se sotto a una finestra	or if you hear someone
fare all'amor sentite,	making love under a window,
ferite pur, ferrite!	then wound him!
Il mio padron sarà!	It will be my master.
In testa egli ha un cappello	He wears a hat on his head
con candidi pennacchi.	that has white plumes.
Addosso un gran mantello,	There's a large cloak on his shoulder,
e spada al fianco egli ha.	and a sword at his side.
Andate, fate presto!	Go on, go quickly!

Don Giovanni pushes the peasants away to pursue their prey.

Don Giovanni:
Tu sol verrai con me. Noi far dobbiamo il resto, e già vedrai cos'è!

Don Giovanni: *(to Masetto)*
But you come with me! We can do the rest ourselves, and you'll soon see what that is!

Zitto, lascia ch'io senta! Ottimamente: dunque dobbiam ucciderlo?

Quiet, let me listen! Perfect. So why do you want to kill him?

Masetto:
Sicuro!

Masetto:
Certainly!

Don Giovanni:
E non ti basteria rompergli l'ossa, fracassargli le spalle?

Don Giovanni:
Wouldn't it be enough to break his bones and fracture his back?

Masetto:
No, no, voglio ammazzarlo, vo' farlo in cento brani.

Masetto:
No, I want to kill him! I want to tear him into a hundred pieces.

Don Giovanni:
Hai buone armi?

Don Giovanni:
Do you have good weapons?

Masetto:
Cospetto! Ho pria questo moschetto, e poi questa pistola.

Masetto:
Of course! I have this musket, and then this pistol.

Masetto hands the musket and pistol to Don Giovanni.

Don Giovanni:
E poi?

Don Giovanni:
And what else?

Masetto:
Non basta?

Masetto:
Isn't that enough?

Don Giovanni beats Masetto with the flat part of his sword.

Don Giovanni:
Eh, basta certo. Or prendi: questa per la
pistola, questa per il moschetto.

Don Giovanni:
Certainly enough. Now, take this for
the pistol, and this for the musket.

Masetto:
Ahi, ahi! La testa mia!

Masetto: *(crying as he falls to the ground)*
Ay, ay! My head!

Don Giovanni:
Taci, o t'uccido!
Questi per ammazzarlo, questi per farlo in
brani!
Villano, mascalzon! Ceffo da cani!

Don Giovanni:
Quiet, or you'll get killed!
This is for wanting to kill him, and this
for wanting to tear him apart!
Villain, bumpkin! Ugly dog!

Don Giovanni throws the weapons down before Masetto, and then leaves hastily.

Masetto:
Ahi! Ahi! La testa mia! Ahi, ahi! Le spalle e
il petto!

Masetto: *(crying loudly)*
Ay! Ay! My head! Ay, ay! My back!
My chest!

Zerlina:
Di sentire mi parve la voce di Masetto!

Zerlina: *(approaching with a lantern)*
I thought I just heard Masetto's voice!

Masetto:
O Dio, Zerlina mia, soccorso!

Masetto:
Oh god, Zerlina, help me!

Zerlina:
Cosa è stato?

Zerlina:
What happened?

Masetto:
L'iniquo, il scellerato i ruppe l'ossa e i nervi.

Masetto:
That villain and scoundrel broke all my bones.

Zerlina:
Oh poveretta me! Chi?

Zerlina:
Oh dear!! Who?

Masetto:
Leporello! Qualche diavol che somiglia a lui!

Masetto:
Leporello! Or else some devil who
resembles him!

Zerlina:
Crudel! Non te diss'io che con questa tua
pazza gelosia ti ridurresti a qualche brutto
passo?
Dove ti duole?

Zerlina: *(helping Masetto to rise)*
How cruel! Didn't I tell you that
your senseless jealousy would get
you into trouble?
Where does it hurt you?

Masetto:
Qui.

Masetto:
Here.

Zerlina:
E poi?

Zerlina:
Where else?

Masetto:
Qui, e ancora qui!

Masetto:
Here, and also here!

Zerlina:
E poi non ti duol altro?

Zerlina:
And are you hurt anywhere else?

Masetto:
Duolmi un poco questo pie', questo braccio,
e questa mano.

Masetto:
I have some pain in this foot, this arm,
and this hand.

Zerlina:
Via, via, non è gran mal, se il resto è sano.
Vientene meco a casa; purché tu mi
prometta d'essere men geloso, io, io ti
guarirò, caro il mio sposo.

Zerlina:
Oh well, it's not so bad. It'll be back
to health with a little rest. Come
home with me. But now you must
promise me not to be so jealous.

Grazioso
ZERLINA

Ve - drai, ca - ri - no, se sei buo - ni - no,

Vedrai, carino,
se sei buonino,
che bel rimedio
ti voglio dar!

You'll see, my love.
I'll cure you.
You'll see, dearest, if you are good,
I'll give you a beautiful remedy!

È naturale,
non dà disgusto,
e lo speziale
non lo sa far.

It's natural,
not offensive,
and the herbalist
doesn't make it.

È un certo balsamo
ch'io porto addosso,
dare tel posso,
se il vuoi provar.

It's a certain balm
that I carry with me.
If you want to try it
I can give it to you.

Saper vorresti dove mi sta?
Sentilo battere, toccami qua!

Would you like to know where I keep
it? Feel it beating, touch me here!

Zerlina places Masetto's hand on her heart, and then both leave.

ACT II – Scene 2

A dark courtyard before Donna Anna's house. There are three doors.
Leporello, wearing Don Giovanni's hat and cloak, appears with Donna Elvira.

Leporello:
Di molte faci il lume s'avvicina, o mio ben:
stiamo qui un poco finché da noi si scosta.

Leporello:
Lots of torchlights are approaching. My
love, let's stay here awhile until they pass by..

Donna Elvira:
Ma che temi, adorato mio sposo?

Donna Elvira:
What are you so afraid of, my adored
husband?

Leporello:
Nulla, nulla. Certi riguardi, io vo' veder se il
lume è già lontano.
(Ah, come da costei liberarmi?)
Rimanti, anima bella!

Leporello:
Nothing, nothing. I just want to see if the
torchlights are far away.
(How can I free myself from her?)
My love, wait here a moment!

Donna Elvira:

Ah! Non lasciarmi! Sola, sola in buio loco
palpitar il cor mi sento, e m'assale un tal
spavento, che mi sembra di morir.

Donna Elvira:
(as Leporello moves further away)
Oh, don't leave me! Alone, alone here in
this dark place, I feel my heart throbbing.
And I'm overcome by such fear, that I
feel like I'm going to die.

Leporello:
(Più che cerco, men ritrovo questa porta
sciagurata;
Piano, piano, l'ho trovata!
Ecco il tempo di fuggir!)

Leporello: *(groping his way around)*
(The more I search the more difficult to
find that infernal door.
Easy, easy! I've found it!
Now is the time to escape from her!)

In the dark, Leporello finds a door, but then misses it again.

Don Octavio and Donna Anna arrive; she is dressed in mourning clothes.

Don Ottavio:
Tergi il ciglio, o vita mia, e dà calma a tuo
dolore! L'ombra omai del genitore pena avrà
de' tuoi martir.

Don Octavio:
Dry those tears, my love and calm your
grieving! The spirit of your father will be
upset by your agonizing.

Donna Anna:
Lascia almen alla mia pena questo piccolo
ristoro; sol la morte, o mio tesoro, il mio
pianto può finir.

Donna Anna:
At least there is some consolation in my
sorrow. It is only death, my love, that can
end my tears.

Donna Elvira:
Ah dov'è lo sposo mio?

Donna Elvira: *(unseen by the others)*
Oh, where is my husband?

Leporello:
(Se mi trova, son perduto!)

Leporello: *(by the door, also unseen)*
(If she finds me, I'm finished!)

Donna Elvira:
Una porta là vegg'io,

Donna Elvira: *(approaches the door)*
I see a door there.

Leporello:
Cheto, cheto, vo'partir!

Leporello:
Quietly, quietly, here's my chance to leave!

At the door, Leporello is confronted by Masetto and Zerlina.

All surround Leporello, who kneels and hides his face in his cloak.

Zerlina e Masetto:
Ferma, briccone, dove ten vai?

Zerlina and Masetto:
Stop, scoundrel! Where are you going?

Donna Anna e Don Ottavio:
Ecco il fellone! Com'era qua?

Donna Anna and Don Octavio:
Here's the criminal! Why is he here?

Donna Anna, Zerlina, Don Ottavio, Masetto:
Ah, mora il perfido che m'ha tradito!

Donna Anna Zerlina, Don Octavio, Masetto:
Death to this perfidious scoundrel!

Donna Elvira:
È mio marito! Pietà!

Donna Elvira: *(unveils herself)*
He is my husband! Have mercy on him!

Donna Anna, Zerlina, Don Ottavio, Masetto:
È Donna Elvira? Quella ch'io vedo? Appena il credo!
No, no, morrà!

Donna Anna Zerlina, Don Octavio, Masetto:
Is that Donna Elvira? Is that who I see? I can't believe it!
No, no, death to him!

Leporello:
Perdon, perdono, signori miei! Quello io non sono, sbaglia costei! Viver lasciatemi per carità!

Leporello: *(as if crying)*
Forgive me, my lords! She is mistaken. I am not that man! For Heaven's sake, let me live!

All are astonished as Leporello reveals his identity.

Donna Anna, Zerlina, Don Ottavio, Masetto:
Dei! Leporello! Che inganno è questo! Stupido resto! Che mai sarà?

Donna Anna Zerlina, Don Octavio, Masetto:
Gods! Leporello! What a deception this is! I'm astonished! How can this be?

Leporello:
(Mille torbidi pensieri mi s'aggiran per la testa; se mi salvo in tal tempesta, è un prodigio in verità.)

Leporello:
(A thousand turbulent thoughts are spinning in my head. If I escape from such a storm, it will be a true miracle.)

Donna Anna leaves. Leporello tries unsuccessfully to follow.

Donna Anna, Zerlina, Don Ottavio, Masetto:
(Mille torbidi pensieri Mi s'aggiran per la testa:
Che giornata, o stelle, è questa!
Che impensata novità!)

Donna Anna Zerlina, Don Octavio, Masetto:
(A thousand turbulent thoughts are spinning in my head.
Oh heavens, what a day this has become! What an unexpected event!)

Zerlina:
Dunque quello sei tu, che il mio Masetto poco fa crudelmente maltrattasti!

Zerlina: *(furiously to Leporello)*
So it was you, who only a short while ago cruelly maltreated Masetto!

Donna Elvira:
Dunque tu m'ingannasti, o scellerato, spacciandoti con me per Don Giovanni!

Donna Elvira: *(to Leporello)*
So it was you who wickedly deceived me, you rogue, by imitating Don Giovanni!

Don Ottavio:
Dunque tu in questi panni venisti qui per qualche tradimento!

Don Octavio:
So it was you who came here in that disguise to deceive us!

Donna Elvira:
A me tocca punirlo.

Donna Elvira:
Let me punish him.

Zerlina:
Anzi a me.

Zerlina:
Let me do it.

Don Ottavio:
No, no, a me.

Don Octavio:
No, no, let me.

Masetto:
Accoppatelo meco tutti e tre.

Masetto:
Let's all three of us deal with him.

Leporello:
Ah, pietà, signori miei!
Dò ragione a voi, a lei
ma il delitto mio non è.
Il padron con prepotenza,
l'innocenza mi rubò.

Leporello:
Have mercy, my lords!
You are right, and so is she.
But I'm not the guilty one.
My tyrannical master
robbed me of my innocence. *(really?)*

(to Donna Elvira)
Donna Elvira, be compassionate!
You understand that he made me do it!

Donna Elvira, compatite!
Voi capite come andò!

(to Masetto and pointing to Donna Elvira)
This girl will tell you,
that I know nothing about Masetto.

Di Masetto non so nulla,
vel dirà questa fanciulla.

È un oretta circumcirca,
che con lei girando vo.

A voi, signore, non dico niente,
certo timore, certo accidente,
di fuori chiaro, di dentro scuro,
non c'è riparo, la porta, il muro.

Io me ne vado verso quel lato, poi qui celato,
l'affar si sa!
Ma s'io sapeva, fuggìa per qua!

I was going around with her
for an hour or so.

(to Don Octavio)
To you, sir, I say nothing.
Certain fears and certain mishaps
are overtly clear, but obscure inside.
There is no hiding place, the door, the wall
(slyly moving toward the door)
I'll go that way, toward the side, and
then hide there.
But if I only knew how to escape from here!

Leporello runs out quickly.

Donna Elvira:
Ferma, perfido, ferma!

Donna Elvira:
Stop scoundrel! Stop!

Masetto:
Il birbo ha l'ali ai piedi!

Masetto:
The rascal has wings on his feet!

Zerlina:
Con qual arte si sottrasse l'iniquo.

Zerlina:
He got out of here so skillfully.

Don Ottavio:
Amici miei, dopo eccessi sì enormi,
dubitar non possiam che
Don Giovanni non sia l'empio uccisore del
padre di Donn'Anna;
in questa casa per poche ore fermatevi, un
ricorso vo'far a chi si deve, e in pochi istanti
vendicarvi prometto.

Don Octavio:
My friends, after such enormous
offences, we can no longer doubt that
Don Giovanni was the merciless
murderer of Donna Anna's father.
Stay here for a few hours. I'll have
recourse to justice, and I promise that
you will have vengeance very soon.

Così vuole dover, pietade, affetto!

Duty demands it, compassion, and affection!

Donna Elvira, Zerlina and Masetto leave.

Andante grazioso
DON OCTAVIO

Il mio tesoro intanto andate a consolar,
e del bel ciglio il pianto cercate di asciugar.

Ditele che i suoi tortia cendicar io vado;
Che sol di stragi e morti nunzio vogl'io
tornar.

Meanwhile, my dearest treasure, console
yourself, and wipe away the tears from
your beautiful eyes.

I am going to have vengeance against
those who wronged her. I will only
return only when I can announce that
we have been avenged by carnage and
death.

Zerlina, with a razor in her hand, drags Leporello in.

Zerlina:
Restati qua!

Zerlina:
You stay here!

Leporello:
Per carità, Zerlina!

Leporello: *(trying to free himself)*
Zerlina, for heaven's sake!

Zerlina:
Eh! Non c'è carità pei pari tuoi.

Zerlina:
There's no mercy for what you're going to suffer.

Leporello:
Dunque cavar mi vuoi?

Leporello:
Do you want to bury me?

Zerlina:
I capelli, la testa, il cor e gli occhi!

Zerlina:
I'll cut the hair on your head, and gouge out your eyes!

Leporello:
Senti, carina mia!

Leporello: *(trying to dissuade her)*
Listen, my dear!

Zerlina:
Guai se mi tocchi!
Vedrai, schiuma de' birbi,
qual premio n'ha chi le ragazze ingiuria.

Zerlina: *(repelling him)*
Careful not to touch me!
You'll see, you rogue, what gift you'll get from an injured girl.

Leporello:
(Liberatemi, o Dei, da questa furia!)

Leporello:
(Gods, free me from this woman's fury!)

Zerlina:
Masetto, olà, Masetto!
Dove diavolo è ito? Servi! Gente!
Nessun vien, nessun sente.

Zerlina:
Masetto, Masetto!
Where the devil has he gone? Servants!
People! No one comes, no one hears.

Leporello:
Fa piano, per pietà! Non trascinarmi a coda di cavallo!

Leporello: *(a peasant enters)*
Easy, for heaven's sake! Don't drag me like a sack of grain!

Zerlina:
Vedrai, vedrai come finisce il ballo! Presto qua quella sedia!

Zerlina:
You'll see that I haven't even started!
Quickly, here in this seat!

Leporello:
Eccola!

Leporello:
Here!

Zerlina:
Siedi!

Zerlina:
Sit!

Leporello:
Stanco non son.

Leporello:
I'm not tired.

Zerlina:
Siedi, o con queste mani ti strappo il cor e
poi lo getto ai cani.

Zerlina:
Sit, or with these I'll tie you up and
throw you to the dogs.

Leporello:
Siedo, ma tu, di grazia, metti giù quel rasoio
mi vuoi forse sbarbar?

Leporello: *(sits down)*
I'm seated, but for Heaven's sake, put
down that razor. Do you want to shave me?

Zerlina:
Sì, mascalzone! Io sbarbare ti vo' senza
sapone.

Zerlina:
Yes, you rascal! I want to shave you
without soap.

Leporello:
Eterni Dei!

Leporello:
Eternal gods!

Zerlina:
Dammi la man!

Zerlina:
Give me your hand!

Leporello:
La mano?

Leporello:
My hand?

Zerlina:
L'altra!

Zerlina:
Now the other one!

Leporello:
Ma che vuoi farmi?

Leporello:
What do you want to do with me?

Zerlina:
Voglio far, voglio far quello che parmi!

Zerlina:
I want to do; I want to do what pleases me!

Zerlina ties Leporello's hands, assisted by the peasant.

Leporello:
Per queste tue manine candide e tenerelle,
per questa fresca pelle, abbi pietà di me!

Leporello:
Have pity on me! Have mercy on these two
white and tender hands and this soft skin!

Zerlina:
Non v'è pietà, briccone;
son una tigre irata, un aspide, un leone.
No, no, non v'è pietà!

Zerlina:
There is no pity, rogue. I am an inflamed
tiger, an asp, and a lion. No, no, there is
no mercy for you!

Leporello:
Ah! Di fuggir si provi!

Leporello:
Oh! If I could only try to escape!

Zerlina:
Sei morto se ti movi!

Zerlina:
Your dead if you move!

Leporello:
Barbari, ingiusti Dei!
In mano di costei chi capitar mi fe'?

Leporello:
Barbarian, unjust gods! Who would
believe that my fate is in your hands?

Zerlina:
Barbaro traditore! Del tuo padrone il core
avessi qui con te!

Zerlina: *(ties Leporello to the chair)*
Barbarous traitor! You too have your
master's evil heart!

Leporello:
Deh! Non mi stringer tanto, l'anima mia sen va!

Leporello:
Heh! Don't tie me so tight!

Zerlina:
Sen vada o resti, intanto non partirai di qua!

Zerlina:
Faint or relax, but you won't get away
from here!

Leporello:
Che strette, o Dei, che botte!
E giorno, ovver è notte?
Che scosse di tremuoto!
Che buia oscurità!

Leporello:
So tight, oh gods, what a disaster!
Is it day or is it night?
What shaking and quivering!
What a gloomy execution!

Zerlina:
Di gioia e di diletto sento brillarmi il petto.
Così, così, cogli uomini, così, così si fa!

Zerlina:
I feel sparkles of joy and delight in my
breast. This is the only way to treat men!

Zerlina departs. Leporello is tied in the chair. In desperation, he asks help from the peasant.

Leporello:
Amico, per pietà, un poco d'acqua fresca o
ch'io mi moro!
Guarda un po' come stretto mi legò
l'assassina!

Leporello:
Friend, for mercy's sake, a little fresh
water or I'll die!
Look how tightly that assassin tied me!

After the peasant departs, Leporello struggles to free himself.

Se potessi liberarmi coi denti?
Oh, venga il diavolo a disfar questi gruppi!

Io vo' veder di rompere la corda come è
forte!
Paura della morte!
E tu, Mercurio, protettor de' ladri,
proteggi un galantuomo coraggio!

Could I free myself by using my teeth?
Or, maybe the devil will come to cut these
cords!
Let me see how strong the cord is, and if
I can break it!
I fear that I'm going to die
And you, Mercury, protector of robbers,
assist a gallant and courageous man!

Leporello pulls hard. The window, to which the cord was fastened, falls.

Bravo! Pria che costei ritorni bisogna dar di
sprone alle calcagna, e trascinar, se occorre
una montagna.

Great! Before they return, I'll need spurs
on my heels to run and cross the
mountain.

Leporello escapes, dragging the chair and window with him.

Zerlina enters, with Donna Elvira, Masetto and peasants.

Zerlina:
Andiam, andiam, Signora! Vedrete in qual
maniera ho concio il scellerato.

Zerlina:
Madam! Let's go and see how I
punished the scoundrel.

Donna Elvira:
Ah! Sopra lui si sfoghi il mio furore!

Donna Elvira:
Oh! You have vented my fury on him!

Zerlina:
Stelle! In qual modo si salvò il briccone?

Zerlina:
Heavens! How could the scoundrel have
escaped?

Donna Elvira:
L'avrà sottratto l'empio suo padrone.

Donna Elvira:
He has stolen the villainy of his master.

Zerlina:
Fu desso senza fallo: anche di questo
informiam Don Ottavio; a lui si spetta far
per noi tutti, o domandar vendetta!

Zerlina:
You're absolutely right! We must inform
Don Octavio about this. He wants to
exact revenge for all of us.

Masetto and the peasants leave.

Donna Elvira:
In quali eccessi, o Numi, in quai misfatti
orribili, tremendi è avvolto il sciagurato!
Ah no! Non puote tardar l'ira del cielo, la
giustizia tardar.
Sentir già parmi la fatale saetta, che gli
piomba sul capo!
Aperto veggio il baratro mortal!
Misera Elvira!
Che contrasto d'affetti, in sen ti nasce!
Perchè questi sospiri?
E queste ambascie?

Donna Elvira:
Oh gods, this wretch is involved in such
horrible and tremendous excesses!

Oh no! Heaven's anger cannot be
delayed, or justice postponed!
I already feel the fatal thunderbolt falling
on his head!
I see the deadly abyss open!
Poor Elvira!
What conflicting emotions have emerged
in your heart! Why these sighs?
Why this anguish?

God &
Devil

Allegro assai
DONNA ELVIRA

Mi tra - dì quell' al - ma in gra - ta,   quell' al - ma in - gra - ta,

Mi tradì, quell'alma ingrata, infelice, o Dio,
mi fa.
Ma tradita e abbandonata, provo ancor per
lui pietà.

Oh god, that ungrateful soul betrayed me
and has made me unhappy.
But even though he betrayed and
abandoned me, I still feel pity for him.

Forgiveness

Quando sento il mio tormento, di vendetta il
cor favella, ma se guardo il suo cimento,
palpitando il cor mi va.

When I feel my anguish, my heart cries
out for vengeance. But if I realize he is
in jeopardy, my heart starts throbbing for him.

ACT II - Scene 3

A walled cemetery with several statues, among them, a statue of the Commandant.
Don Giovanni leaps over the wall, still wearing Leporello's hat.

Don Giovanni:
Ah, ah, ah, questa è buona, or lasciala
cercar; che bella notte!
È più chiara del giorno, sembra fatta
per gir a zonzo a caccia di ragazze.

È tardi? Oh, ancor non sono due della notte;
Avrei voglia un po' di saper come è finito
l'affar tra Leporello e Donna Elvira, s'egli
ha avuto giudizio!

Leporello:
Alfin vuole ch'io faccia un precipizio.

Don Giovanni:
(È desso.) Oh, Leporello!

Leporello:
Chi mi chiama?
Don Giovanni:
Non conosci il padron?

Leporello:
Così non conoscessi!

Don Giovanni:
Come, birbo?

Leporello:
Ah, siete voi? Scusate!

Don Giovanni:
Cosa è stato?

Leporello:
Per cagion vostra io fui quasi accoppato.

Don Giovanni: *(laughing)*
Ha, ha, ha, this is good. Now let her try
to find me!
What a beautiful night! It's brighter than
the day; and seems to urge me to rove
about and hunt for pretty girls.
Is it late? Oh, it's not yet two in the
morning. I would really like to know how
things went with Leporello and Donna
Elvira, and if he was successful with her!

Leporello: *(from behind the wall)*
Surely, he wishes to ruin me!

Don Giovanni:
(That's him.) Oh, Leporello!

Leporello:
Who's calling me?
Don Giovanni:
Don't you recognize your master?

Leporello:
I wish I never knew him!

Don Giovanni:
What did you say, you rogue?

Leporello:
Oh, is that you? Excuse me!

Don Giovanni:
What happened?

Leporello:
Because of you, I was almost killed.

Don Giovanni:
Ebben, non era questo un onore per te?

Don Giovanni:
Well, wasn't that an honor for you?

Leporello:
Signor, vel dono.

Leporello:
Sir, you can have the honor.

Don Giovanni:
Via, via, vien qua! Che belle cose ti deggio dir.

Don Giovanni:
Come, come this way! I've some great things to tell you!

Leporello:
Ma cosa fate qui?

Leporello:
But what are you doing here?

Don Giovanni:
Vien dentro e lo saprai. Diverse storielle che accadute mi son da che partisti, ti dirò un'altra volta: or la più bella ti vo'solo narrar.

Don Giovanni:
Come inside and you'll find out. Several things happened to me since you were away. I'll tell you another time, but the best one I'll tell you now.

Leporello climbs over the wall and exchanges hat and cloak with Don Giovanni.

Leporello:
Donnesca al certo?

Leporello:
Is it about women?

Don Giovanni:
C'è dubbio? Una fanciulla, bella, giovin, galante, per la strada incontrai; le vado appresso, la prendo per la man, fuggir mi vuole; dico poche parole, ella mi piglia, sai per chi?

Don Giovanni:
Do you doubt it? I met a charming and beautiful young girl while I was on the road. I approached her, but when I took her hand, she tried to run away. After a few words she took me for. Whom do you think?

Leporello:
Non lo so.

Leporello:
I don't know.

Don Giovanni:
Per Leporello!

Don Giovanni:
For Leporello!

Leporello:
Per me?

Leporello:
For me?

Don Giovanni:
Per te.

Don Giovanni:
For you.

Leporello:
Va bene.

Leporello:
Good.

Don Giovanni:
Per la mano essa allora mi prende.

Don Giovanni:
Then she took me by the hand.

Leporello:
Ancora meglio.

Leporello:
Even better.

Don Giovanni:
M'accarezza, mi abbraccia:
"Caro il mio Leporello! Leporello, mio caro!"
Allor m'accorsi ch'era qualche tua bella.

Don Giovanni:
She kissed me, she embraced me: "My dearest Leporello! Leporello, my dear!" Then I realized that she was one of your girls.

Leporello:
(Oh maledetto!)

Leporello:
(Damn it!)

Don Giovanni:
Dell'inganno approfitto; non so come mi riconosce, grida; sento gente, a fuggire mi metto, e pronto pronto per quel muretto in questo loco io monto.

Don Giovanni:
I took advantage of it. Unfortunately, somehow she recognized me and began to shout. People approached and then it was time to run away. So quick as light, I jumped here over this wall.

Leporello:
E mi dite la cosa con tanta indifferenza?

Leporello:
And why do you tell this to me so casually?

Don Giovanni:
Perché no?

Don Giovanni:
Why not?

Leporello:
Ma se fosse costei stata mia moglie?

Leporello:
But what if that pretty girl was my wife?

Don Giovanni:
Meglio ancora!

Don Giovanni: *(laughing loudly)*
Even better! Ass!

The moon breaks through the clouds, casting light on the Statue of the Commandant. Then the Statue speaks.

La Statua:
Di rider finirai pria dell'aurora!

The Statue:
Your laughter will end before dawn! Random!

Don Giovanni:
Chi ha parlato?

Don Giovanni:
Who spoke?

Leporello:
Ah! Qualche anima sarà dell'altro mondo, che vi conosce a fondo.

Leporello: *(in extreme fear)*
Oh, some ghost from another world, who recognizes you well.

Don Giovanni:

Taci, sciocco! Chi va là?

Don Giovanni:
(striking some statues with his sword)
Quiet, you fool! Who goes there?

La Statua:
Ribaldo, audace! Lascia a' morti la pace!

The Statue:
Insolent rogue! Let the dead sleep in peace!

Leporello:
Ve l'ho detto!

Leporello: *(trembling)*
I told you!

Don Giovanni:
Sarà qualcun di fuori che si burla di noi!

Don Giovanni:
It's someone outside playing a joke on us!

Ehi, del Commendatore non è questa la
statua? Leggi un poco quella iscrizion.

(with indifference and contempt)
Hey, isn't that the statue of the
Commandant? Read me the inscription.

Leporello:
Scusate. Non ho imparato a leggere ai raggi
della luna.

Leporello:
Excuse me: I never learned to read by
moonlight.

Don Giovanni:

Leggi, dico!

Don Giovanni:
(grasps his sword to threaten Leporello)
Read it!

Leporello:
"Dell'empio che mi trasse al passo estremo
qui attendo la vendetta."
Udiste? Io tremo!

Leporello: *(reads the inscription)*
"Here, I await vengeance upon the evil
man who ended my life."
Did you hear that? I'm trembling!

Don Giovanni:
O vecchio buffonissimo! Digli che questa
sera l'attendo a cenar meco!

Don Giovanni:
You old buffoon! Tell him that I expect
him to join me for dinner tonight!

Leporello:
Che pazzia ! Ma vi par, oh Dei, mirate, che
terribili occhiate egli ci dà! Par vivo! Par che
senta, e che voglia parlar!

Leporello:
What madness! I won't. Oh heavens, look
at how sternly he glares at us! He seems
alive! He seems to hear! He wants to speak!

Don Giovanni:
Orsù, va là! O qui t'ammazzo, e poi ti
seppellisco!

Don Giovanni:
Go on! Or I'll kill you, and then bury
you!

Leporello:
Piano, piano, signore, ora ubbidisco.
O statua gentilissima del gran Commendatore.
Padron! Mi trema il core, non posso
terminar!

Leporello:
Master, easy, easy. As you please.
Oh, most illustrious statue of the great
Commandant. Master! My heart is
trembling, I can't go on!

Don Giovanni:
Finiscila, o nel petto ti metto questo acciar!

Don Giovanni:
Finish it, or I'll put this steel through
your heart!

Leporello:
(Che impiccio, che capriccio!)

Leporello:
(What a mess! What a caprice!)

Don Giovanni:
(Che gusto! Che spassetto!)

Leporello:
Io sentomi gelar!

Don Giovanni:
Lo voglio far tremar!

Leporello:
O statua gentillissima, benchè di marmo
siate. Ah padron mio! Mirate! Che seguita a
guardar!

Don Giovanni:

Mori!

Leporello:
No, no, attendete! Signor, il padron mio,
badate ben, non io, vorria con voi cenar! Ah
che scena è questa!

Oh ciel! Chinò la testa!

Don Giovanni:
Va là, che sei un buffone!
Leporello:
Guardate ancor, padrone!

Don Giovanni:
E che degg'io guardar?

Leporello:
Colla marmorea testa, ei fa così, così!

Don Giovanni e Leporello:

Colla marmorea testa, ei fa così, così!

Don Giovanni:
Parlate, se potete! Verrete a cena?

La Statua:
Sì!

Leporello:
Mover mi posso, appena, mi manca, o Dei,
la lena! Per carità, partiamo, partiamo via di
qua! Andiamo via di qua!

Don Giovanni:
(What fun! What amusement!)

Leporello:
I feel a chill!

Don Giovanni:
I want to make him tremble!

Leporello:
Oh, most illustrious statue, even though
you are of marble. Master! Look! His
eyes are glowing!

Don Giovanni:
(advances menacingly toward the Statue)
Die!

Leporello:
No, wait! *(to the Statue)* My lord, my
master, not I, would like to dine with
you! What a scene this is!
(the Statue nods in approval)
Oh heavens! He nodded his head!

Don Giovanni: *(not looking at the Statue)*
You're a buffoon!
Leporello:
Master, look again!

Don Giovanni:
What should I look at?

Leporello: *(imitating the statue)*
He goes like this with his marble head!

Don Giovanni and Leporello:
(the statue bends its head)
He goes like this with his marble head!

Don Giovanni: *(to the Statue)*
Speak if you can! Will you come to dinner?

The Statue: *(inclining its head)*
Yes!

Leporello:
I can hardly move. I have no strength.
For mercy's sake, let's go! For heaven's
sake, let's leave! Let's leave here! Let's go!

Don Giovanni:
Bizzarra è inver la scena, verrà il buon
vecchio a cena a prepararla andiamo,
partiamo via di qua!
Andiamo via di qua!

Don Giovanni:
The scene is indeed bizarre. The old man
will come to dinner. Let's go and prepare
dinner. Let's leave here!
Let's go!

ACT II – Scene 4

A room in Donna Anna's house.

Don Ottavio:
Calmatevi, idol mio! Di quel ribaldo vedrem
puniti in breve i gravi eccessi, vendicati
sarem.

Don Octavio:
Be calm, my love! Soon this libertine
shall be punished for his grave excesses.
We shall be avenged.

Donna Anna:
Ma il padre, o Dio!

Donna Anna:
Oh god, my poor father!

Don Ottavio:
Convien chinare il ciglio al volere del ciel.
Respira, o cara! Di tua perdita amara fia
doman, se vuoi, dolce compenso, questo cor,
questa mano, che il mio tenero amor.

Don Octavio:
But we must bow our heads to the will
of heaven. Rest my dear! For tomorrow
your bitter loss will be sweetly rewarded
by my tender love, my heart, and my hand.

Donna Anna:
O dei, che dite in sì tristi momenti?

Donna Anna:
What do you talk about at such sad
moments?

Don Ottavio:
E che? Vorresti con indugi novelli accrescer
le mie pene? Ah! Crudele!

Don Octavio:
What? Do you want to increase my pain
with renewed postponements? Oh, you
are so cruel!

Donna Anna:
Crudele? Ah no, giammai mio ben! Troppo
mi spiace allontanarti un ben che
lungamente la nostr'alma desia.
Ma il mondo, o Dio!

Donna Anna:
Cruel? Oh, no, my love! I regret so
much that I must turn you away from a
happiness our souls have long desired.
Oh god, it is this horrible world!

Non sedur la costanza del sensibil mio core;
ahbastanza per te mi parla amore!

Do not tempt the faithfulness of my
sensitive heart! It is enough for you that
love speaks to me!

Larghetto
DONNA ANNA

Non   mi   dir,   bell' - i   -   dol   mi -   o,

Non mi dir, bell'idol mio, che son io crudel con te.

Don't tell me, my dear love, that I am cruel to you.

Tu ben sai quant'io t'amai, tu conosci la mia fè!
Calma, calma il tuo tormento, se di duol non vuoi ch'io mora! Forse un giorno il cielo ancora sentirà pietà di me!

You know well how much I have loved you, and you know my faith!
Calm your torment if you do not want me to die of sorrow! Perhaps one day, heaven will yet feel mercy for me!

(Donna Anna exits)

Don Ottavio:
Ah si segua il suo passo; io vo' con lei dividere i martiri.
Saran meco men gravi i suoi sospiri

Don Octavio:
Ah! Let me follow her footsteps. I'll share her grieving.
Her sorrows will be less if she shares them with me.

ACT II – Scene 5

A large illuminated hall. A sumptuous banquet has been prepared.

Don Giovanni:
Già la mensa è preparata. Voi suonate, amici cari!
Giacché spendo i miei danari, io mi voglio divertir. Leporello, questa tavola!

Don Giovanni:
The table is already prepared. Play music, dear friends!
Since I'm spending my money, I want to enjoy myself. Leporello, serve!

Leporello:
Son prontissimo a servir.

Leporello:
Sir, I'm ready to serve.

The musicians play a melody from Martin's "Una cosa rara."

Leporello:
Bravi! "Cosa rara!"

Leporello:
Terrific! "Cosa rara!"

Don Giovanni:
Che ti par del bel concerto?

Don Giovanni:
How do you like the concert?

Leporello:
È conforme al vostro merto.

Leporello:
It's consistent with your excellence.

Don Giovanni:
Ah che piatto saporito!

Don Giovanni:
Such delicious food!

Leporello:
(Ah che barbaro appetito!
Che bocconi da gigante!
Mi par proprio di svenir!)

Leporello:
(Such a barbarous appetite!
What gigantic mouthfuls!
I think I'm going to faint from hunger!)

Don Giovanni:
(Nel veder i miei bocconi
gli par proprio di svenir.)
Piatto!

Don Giovanni:
(Watching my mouthfuls, I think he's
going to faint from hunger.)
Another plate here!

Leporello:
Servo.

Leporello:
I'll serve it to you.

The musicians begin to play Paisiello's "Fra I due litiganti il terzo gode."

Evvivano "I litiganti."

Cheers for "The litigants."

Don Giovanni:
Versa il vino! Eccellente marzimino!

Don Giovanni:
Pour more wine! Excellent red wine!

Leporello:
(Questo pezzo di fagiano, piano piano
vo'inghiottir.)

Leporello:
(I'll eat this piece of pheasant quietly.)

Don Giovanni:
(Sta mangiando, quel marrano! Fingerò di
non capir.)

Don Giovanni:
(That rascal is eating! I'll pretend not to
see.)

The musicians play music from Mozart's "The Marriage of Figaro."

Leporello:
Questa poi la conosco pur troppo.

Leporello:
I know this one too well.

Don Giovanni:
Leporello!

Don Giovanni: *(ignoring Leporello)*
Leporello!

Leporello:
Padron mio!

Leporello: *(with his mouth full)*
Yes, my master!

Don Giovanni:
Parla schietto, mascalzone.

Don Giovanni:
Speak more clearly, you rogue.

Leporello:
Non mi lascia una flussione le parole proferir.

Leporello: *(clearing his throat)*
My mouth is hoarse.

Don Giovanni:
Mentre io mangio fischia un poco.

Don Giovanni:
Whistle a little something while I'm eating.

Leporello:
Non so far.

Leporello:
I don't know how to whistle.

Don Giovanni:
Cos'è?

Don Giovanni: *(looking at Leporello)*
What's that you say?

Leporello:
Scusate! Sì eccellente è il vostro cuoco, che
lo volli anch'io provar.

Don Giovanni:
(Sì eccellente è il cuoco mio, che lo volle
anch'ei provar.)

Donna Elvira:
L'ultima prova dell'amor mio ancor vogl'io
fare con te. Più non rammento gl'inganni
tuoi, pietade io sento.

Don Giovanni e Leporello:
Cos'è?

Donna Elvira:

Da te non chiede quest'alma oppressa della
sua fede qualche mercè.

Leporello:
Excuse me! Your cook is so wonderful
that I wanted to taste it too.

Don Giovanni:
(Yes, my cook is so excellent, that he
wanted to taste it too.)

Donna Elvira: *(entering desperately)*
I want to make the last test of my love
for you. I will forget your betrayals. I will
be merciful to you.

Don Giovanni and Leporello:
What is this?

Donna Elvira:
(kneeling before Don Giovanni)
This injured soul asks mercy from you.

Thunder is heard from an approaching storm.

Don Giovanni:
Mi maraviglio! Cosa volete?
Se non sorgete non resto in piè.

Donna Elvira:
Ah non deridere gli affani miei!

Leporello:
(Quasi da piangere mi fa costei.)

Don Giovanni:
Io te deridere? Cielo, e perché?
Che vuoi, mio bene?

Donna Elvira:
Che vita cangi!

Don Giovanni:
Brava!

Donna Elvira:
Cor perfido!

Don Giovanni:
Lascia ch'io mangi, e se ti piace, mangia con
me.

Don Giovanni: *(trying to raise her)*
I am amazed! What do you want?
If you don't rise, I'll kneel with you.

Donna Elvira:
Don't mock my anguish!

Leporello:
(She almost makes me cry.)

Don Giovanni: *(raising Elvira tenderly)*
Would I mock you? Heavens, why?
What is it you want, my love?

Donna Elvira:
That you change your life!

Don Giovanni:
Excellent!

Donna Elvira:
Faithless heart!

Don Giovanni: *(sitting down at the table)*
Let me eat. And if you wish, join me.

Donna Elvira:
Rèstati, barbaro! Nel lezzo immondo
esempio orribile d'iniquità!

Donna Elvira: *(disdainfully)*
Barbarian! Then remain in your indec
filth and dreadful wickedness!

Don Giovanni:
Vivan le femmine.
Viva il buon vino!
Sostegno e gloria d'umanità!

Don Giovanni: *(raising his glass)*
Here's to women!
Here's to good wine!
They are the nourishment and glory of
humanity!

Leporello:
(Se non si muove al suo dolore, di sasso ha il
core, o cor non ha.)

Leporello:
(She cannot move him with her
suffering. His heart is of stone, or he has
no heart.)

Donna Elvira rushes out to the door, and becomes terrified when she sees the Statue.
Then she departs through another door.

Donna Elvira:
Ah!

Donna Elvira:
Ah!

Don Giovanni e Leporello:
Che grido è questo mai?

Don Giovanni and Leporello:
What was the reason for that scream?

Don Giovanni:
Va a veder che cosa è stato!

Don Giovanni:
Go and see what happened!

Leporello:
Ah!

Leporello: *(upon seeing the Statue)*
Ah!

Don Giovanni:
Che grido indiavolato!
Leporello, che cos'è?

Don Giovanni:
What a diabolic shout!
Leporello, what is it?

Leporello:
Ah, signor, per carità! Non andate fuor di
qua! L'uom di sasso, l'uomo bianco.
Ah padrone! Io gelo, io manco. Se vedeste
che figura, se sentiste come fa ta ta ta ta!

Leporello: *(in fright)*
Ah, sir, for heaven's sake! Don't go out
there! The man of stone, the man of marble.
Master! I'm chilled, I'm fainting. If you
saw that figure. If you hear his ta ta ta ta!

Don Giovanni:
Non capisco niente affatto. Tu sei matto in
verità.

Don Giovanni:
I don't understand it at all. You're indeed
mad.

There is knocking on the door.

Leporello:
Ah sentite!

Leporello:
Listen!

Don Giovanni:
Qualcun batte! Apri!

Don Giovanni:
Someone's knocking! Open it!

Leporello:
Io tremo!

Leporello:
I'm trembling!

Don Giovanni:
Apri, dico!

Don Giovanni:
Open the door!

Leporello:
Ah!

Leporello:
No!

Don Giovanni:
Matto! Per togliermi d'intrico ad aprir io
stesso andrò.

Don Giovanni:
Idiot! To solve this puzzle I'll go and
open it myself.

Leporello:
(Non vo' più veder l'amico pian pianin
m'asconderò.)

Leporello:
(I'll never see our friend again. I'll
quietly hide.)

Don Giovanni opens the door. Leporello hides under the table.
Amid a clap of thunder, the Statue of the Commandant appears.

La Statua:
Don Giovanni, a cenar teco m'invitasti e son
venuto!

The Statue:
Don Giovanni, you invited me to dine
with you, and I have come!

Don Giovanni:
Non l'avrei giammai creduto; ma farò quel
che potrò. Leporello, un altra cena fa che
subito si porti!

Don Giovanni:
I would never have believed it, but I'll do
what I can. Leporello, another dinner.
Have it brought immediately!

Leporello:
Ah padron! Siam tutti morti!

Leporello: *(peeking from under the table)*
Oh master! We're all going to die!

Don Giovanni:
Vanne dico!

Don Giovanni:
Listen to me!

La Statua:
Ferma un po'! Non si pasce di cibo mortale
chi si pasce di cibo celeste; altra cure più
gravi di queste, altra brama quaggiù mi
guidò!

The Statue:
Stop a moment! No nourishment from
mortal food for one who is nourished by
celestial food. I am guided here by other
cares and cravings that are more solemn
than these!

Leporello:
(La terzana d'avere mi sembra e le membra
fermar più non sò.)

Leporello:
(It's like having a fever. My limbs won't
stop shaking.)

Don Giovanni:
Parla dunque! Che chiedi!
Che vuoi?

Don Giovanni:
Then speak! What do you ask for?
What do you want?

La Statua:
Parlo; ascolta! Più tempo non ho!

The Statue:
I'll speak and you listen! I have little time!

Don Giovanni:
Parla, parla, ascoltando ti sto.

Don Giovanni: *(angrily and defiantly)*
Then speak. I am listening to you.

La Statua:
Tu m'invitasti a cena, il tuo dover or sai.
Rispondimi: verrai tu a cenar meco?

The Statue:
You invited me to dinner. You now
know your duty. Answer me: will you
come to dine with me?

Leporello:
Oibò; tempo non ha, scusate.

Leporello: *(trembling from far away)*
Make an excuse. Tell him you have no time now.

Don Giovanni:
A torto di viltate tacciato mai sarò!

Don Giovanni: *(calmly and coldly)*
I shall never be accused of cowardice!

La Statua:
Risolvi!

The Statue: *(impatiently)*
Then decide!

Don Giovanni:
Ho già risolto!

Don Giovanni:
I have decided!

La Statua:
Verrai?

The Statue:
Will you come?

Leporello:
Dite di no!

Leporello: *(to Don Giovanni)*
Say no!

Don Giovanni:
Ho fermo il cuore in petto: non ho timor:
verrò!

Don Giovanni:
My heart is beating steadily. I'm not
afraid. I'll come!

La Statua:
Dammi la mano in pegno!

The Statue: *(offering his left hand)*
Give me your hand as a pledge!

Don Giovanni:
Eccola! Ohimé!

Don Giovanni: *(offering his right hand)*
Here it is! Let go!

La Statua:
Cos'hai?

The Statue:
What is it?

Don Giovanni:
Che gelo è questo mai?

Don Giovanni:
What is this deadly coldness?

La Statua:
Pentiti, cangia vita.
È l'ultimo momento!

The Statue:
Repent and change your life!
This is your last chance!

Don Giovanni:
No, no, ch'io non mi pento. Vanne lontan da me!

Don Giovanni: *(vainly tries to free himself)*
No, no, I won't repent! Get far away from me!

La Statua:
Pentiti, scellerato!

The Statue:
Repent, you scoundrel!

Don Giovanni:
No, vecchio infatuato!

Don Giovanni:
No, old fool!

La Statua:
Pentiti!

The Statue:
Repent!

Don Giovanni:
No!

Don Giovanni:
No!

La Statua:
Sì!

The Statue:
Yes!

Don Giovanni:
No!

Don Giovanni:
No!

La Statua:
Ah! Tempo più non v'è!

The Statue:
There is no more time!

As the Statue disappears, the earth trembles, and flames rise from all sides.

Don Giovanni:
Da qual tremore insolito sento assalir gli spiriti! Dond'escono quei vortici di foco pien d'orror?

Don Giovanni:
What strange fears! I feel the spirits assailing me! Where have those whirlpools of fire and terror come from?

Coro di diavoli:
Tutto a tue colpe è poco!
Vieni, c'è un mal peggior!

Chorus of Devils: *(from below)*
It is too little punishment for your sins!
Come, there is even worse for you!

Don Giovanni:
Chi l'anima mi lacera!
Chi m'agita le viscere!
Che strazio, ohimé, che smania!
Che inferno, che terror!

Don Giovanni:
They rip my soul!
They agitate my insides!
What torture, what delirium!
What hell! What terror!

Leporello:
(Che ceffo disperato! Che gesti da dannato!
Che gridi, che lamenti! Come mi fa terror!)

Leporello:
(What desperate cries! What noise from the damned! What shouts, what laments! How if fills me with terror!)

Don Giovanni:
Ah!

Don Giovanni: *(the flames engulf him)*
Ah!

Leporello:
Ah!

Leporello:
Ah!

ACT II – Scene 6

Donna Anna, Donna Elvira, Zerlina, Don Octavio and Masetto,
accompanied by ministers of justice.

Donna Elvira, Zerlina, Don Ottavio e Masetto:
Ah, dov'è il perfido?
Dov'è l'indegno?
Tutto il mio sdegno sfogar io vo'!

Donna Elvira, Zerlina, Don Octavio and Masetto:
Where is that perfidious man?
Where is that contemptible man?
I want to unleash all of my anger!

Donna Anna:
Solo mirandolo stretto in catene alle mie pene calma darò.

Donna Anna:
My pain can only be calmed if I see him bound in chains.

Leporello:
Più non sperate di ritrovarlo, più non cercate. Lontano andò.

Leporello: *(pale and trembling)*
Don't expect to see him again. Search no more. He's gone far away.

Tutti:
Cos'è? Favella! Via presto, sbrigati!

All:
What is it? Tell us! Hurry up!

Leporello:
Venne un colosso.

Leporello:
A gigantic statue came.

Tutti:
Via presto, sbrigati!

All:
Tell us! Hurry up!

Leporello:
Ma se non posso. Tra fumo e fuoco. Badate un poco. L'uomo di sasso... Fermate il passo. Giusto là sotto, diede il gran botto. Giusto là il diavolo. Sel trangugiò!

Leporello:
But I can't go on. Listen a moment. It was amidst smoke and fire. The man of stone... He seized him. Just there in the ground, he gave the great blow. The devil swallowed him up and he vanished!

Tutti:
Stelle, che sento!

All:
Heavens, what do I hear!

Leporello:
Vero è l'evento!

Leporello:
It's all quite true!

Donna Elvira:
Ah, certo è l'ombra che m'incontrò.

Donna Elvira:
It must have been the ghost I met.

Donna Anna, Zerlina, Don Ottavio e Masetto:
Ah, certo è l'ombra che l'incontrò.

Donna Anna, Zerlina, Don Octavio and Masetto:
It must have been the ghost she met.

Don Ottavio:
Or che tutti, o mio tesoro, vendicati siam dal cielo. Porgi, porgi a me un ristoro, non mi far languire ancor.

Donna Anna:
Lascia, o caro, un anno ancora allo sfogo del mio cor.

Don Ottavio:
Al desio di chi m'adora ceder deve un fido amor.

Donna Anna:
Al desio di chi t'adora ceder deve un fido amor.

Donna Elvira:

Io men vado in un ritiro a finir la vita mia!

Zerlina:
Noi, Masetto, a casa andiamo! A cenar in compagnia!

Masetto:
Noi, Zerlina, a casa andiamo! A cenar in compagnia!

Leporello:
Ed io vado all'osteria a trovar padron miglior.

Zerlina, Masetto e Leporello:
Resti dunque quel birboncon Proserpina e Pluton.
E noi tutti, o buona gente, ripetiam allegramente l'antichissima canzon.

Tutti:
Questo è il fin di chi fa mal; e de' perfidi la morte alla vita è sempre ugual.

Don Octavio: *(to Donna Anna)*
My treasure, now that all of us are vindicated by heaven, console me, and don't let me languish any more.

Donna Anna:
My dear, let another year pass for my grief to run its course.

Don Octavio:
A faithful love must submit to the desires of one who adores him.

Donna Anna: *(offers Octavio her hand)*
A faithful love must submit to the desires of one whom he loves.

Donna Elvira:
(to Donna Anna and Don Octavio)
I'll go into a convent for the rest of my life!

Zerlina:
Masetto, let's go home and dine together!

Masetto:
Zerlina, let's go home and dine together!

Leporello:
And I'm going to the inn to find a better master.

Zerlina, Masetto and Leporello:
Let the scoundrel remain with Persephene and Pluto.
And now good people, let's all repeat the old, old song again.

All:
This is how all evildoers end. All the wicked die as they have lived.

End of opera